BUILDING A DREAM TEAM

*Battling from one foot in the grave
to creating an innovative,
collaborative company*

Kelly Hager

Contributing writer: Richard H. Weiss
Book design by LaVidaCo Communications
Cover design by Jordan Alsobrook

Thanks to my family, my amazing sisterhood and leadership team, all members of The Kelly Hager Group, the most wonderful friends a girl could ask for, and the people who became my speed bumps along the way.

As a true entrepreneur, I'm looking forward to where my life goes from here.

Contents

Kelly Hager

Introduction

Not everyone gets a near-death experience. I was one of the lucky ones.

On July 1, 2010 I had one foot in the grave. While the rest of the world was focused on the BP oil spill disaster which had just become the worst oceanic spill in U.S. history, I didn't know it, but I was about to be in for the fight of my life.

Fast forward to late August and you could have started shoveling dirt on me and I would have been none the wiser. I was in ICU, comatose with my organs shutting down.

I had always been told you were supposed to see God at moments like that.

Didn't happen.

Huge disappointment.

Maybe that's why I'm still here. Like my family, I have high expectations and assume people will step up in moments of crisis, God included. So maybe I was too pissed off to die. Of course, that's just a guess. Like I said… comatose.

Not long after I finally came around, my husband told me he wanted a divorce.

Still, I had survived. This my family and friends could celebrate. But no one expected me to thrive. I had to learn to focus again, see again, walk again, read again, and become a single mom for the first time. I had to come to grips with and grieve over the fact that waffle irons, as handy and useful as they appear, cannot under any circumstances be used to extract catheters (more about this later).

I was helpless.

It was the best thing that ever happened to me. Just what the doctor ordered, or should have ordered.

For up to that point, I was Kelly Mittelman Hager, a driven and successful entrepreneur and real estate agent, but neither an entirely happy nor an entirely whole person.

Today I am both—all in and all here. I am more successful professionally than I have ever been. Even more importantly, I have found my place and my purpose in the world.

It was a process that started with being helpless and recognizing that the only thing that you will ever really do alone is die.

The rest is all part of a big collaboration, at first with your parents who bring you into the world and show you how it goes, then increasingly it's with others. My dear mother, who I didn't give the credit she deserved before I was sick, has been by my side and is my lifeline to this day.

At this writing, I am 42. If all goes according to the actuarial tables, I'm half-baked, parboiled. So the first half was all about learning, experimenting, succeeding somewhat, but missing the point.

The second half is about getting the point, recognizing what it takes and going there. The point is this:

You can have it all. But you cannot do it alone. Oh, and by the way, did I mention you have to have the guts to do it? Anything worth fighting for is never easy.

Over the last four years, post-coma, with a large group effort, we have taken our real estate business from $10 million to $53+ million in annual sales. We've developed a very non-traditional team model, where everyone truly supports each other. We came across a word from a local marketing company and used it with our staff. I said I wanted to *empowergize* them. I wanted them to accept my vision and feed off of my passion, but also give them the opportunity to implement the strategies and deliver against the vision. This they have done.

The beginning of our success came during one of the most difficult real estate markets in recent times (and the market still isn't perfect). So I've just got to say, it pays to be helpless, at least for a minute.

Despite our success, I'm not going to pretend this book is the answer to your prayers. I'm not a billionaire. Nor am I an oracle. If you picked up this book and passed up others on the shelf nearby, it might be because you found it hard to relate to those soothsayers. Maybe Donald Trump has good advice for you, but he really is a breed of his own. Maybe Suze Orman knows what she's talking about, but it isn't all about the Benjamins. And maybe you simply have had your fill of Dr. Phil.

This book is written for you. I imagine if you picked it up, you saw something of yourself in me. You work hard. You are smart. You are creative. You are an unfinished bit of business.

Here's what I hope you are thinking: If someone like Kelly can emerge from a coma and find financial success and happiness, then maybe I, coherent and sitting upright at this moment, can do even better.

At this time in your life, you may feel lost and confused. Even worse, you may be feeling satisfied and content.

Whenever I found myself in those places, my dad, a firebreather, would notice. He would bark at me, "Put your war paint on, Kelly. Get busy."

I hope by the time you turn the last page of this book, you will be doing just that.

Kelly Mittelman Hager

January 2015

1

Raised on Risk

I was a difficult child. I got lousy grades. Making friends was a challenge. You could have said all of those things about me. Yet, I could also be remembered this way: I overcame a learning disability, created and led my own peer group, and made my parents proud.

In short, I am a success story. It just took a long time to get there. In looking back, I recognize that I often fought my biggest battles not with my enemies, but the people who loved me. Did I tell you I'm stubborn, very stubborn?

Hey, I came by that trait honestly. Born with it. In the blood.

Meet my parents.

Terry and Allen Mittelman, what a pair. They were the founders of The Library, Ltd., a bookstore in St. Louis, Missouri. They had few close friends, other than each other. They shared a very powerful vision, and complimented each other's abilities and temperaments. A colleague who worked with them at the bookstore referred to them as a Society of Two.

My dad had a tough childhood. He grew up in tenement housing near the Bowery in New York. The son of Sol and Violet Mittelman, he often found a drunk dozing in the landing when he came home from school. As he tried to sleep each night, he would hear the Third Avenue El (an elevated train) rumble past his window. Money was very tight, not much for extras. His mom returned to work when his father became ill; my dad had a lot of unsupervised time on his hands. Fortunately, he had a role model in his grandpa, Sam, who lived with the family and ran a hand laundry. Sam went to work early every day, arriving home often after dark, and smelling of starch. He became president of the hand launderers association. My dad had such fond memories of his grandpa; he saved him many times from family trials and tribulations. Sam's example of hard work motivated my dad strongly. If there's one thing you could say about my dad, he was driven.

Money never meant all that much to my dad. He made a lot of it over the years, first in card games where he won big pots from men much older than he, then in business. The money was nice, but it was simply one way of keeping score. What he focused on was success, taking the hand you were dealt and playing your cards right. I was lucky to inherit that risk-taking trait from him.

My mom grew up in another world, a comfortable suburb in St. Louis. Her dad, Elmer Gidlow, and her grandfather, Herman Glick, were partners in a quite successful residential real estate business. Her parents gave her everything she wanted or needed. She was the apple of her daddy's eye. That apple wasn't just metaphorical. Elmer would take the first bite out of a crisp Granny Smith to spare my mom's delicate teeth.

As good and kind as they were, and they were profoundly wonderful grandparents, Elmer and my grandma Selma, expected less from my mom than from her brothers. In the 1950s, many women were expected to get their educations and settle in as housewives, moms, and community volunteers. When it came to careers, Elmer focused on his two sons. My Uncle David moved to California and was responsible for the sourcing and manufacturing of clothing for various large corporations and spent much of his time overseas.

My Uncle Jerome stayed in St. Louis, graduated from Washington University, and landed in commercial real estate. I guess it could be said real estate is in my DNA.

In those days, my grandparents' expectation was that my mom attend college and become a teacher. They felt teaching would give her flexibility; she could have that traditional family life and be home for the kids after school and during the summer and breaks.

My mom headed down that road. She took some education courses at the University of Oklahoma and nearly died of boredom. She came home, enrolled in Washington University's business school, one of very few women to do so in the 1960s, and never looked back. Professors teased her that she was husband shopping. Not funny, she told them, and they backed off.

By this time, Selma and Elmer knew Terry was not going down a traditional path, and only felt more so when she took off for London to participate in a business exchange program where she worked for the National Coal Board. After returning to the United States, she didn't go home but to New York, and got into retailing. That's where she met my dad.

He was short, all of five feet, six inches, nine years older than my mom, and fastidious; the kind of guy who arranged his shirts by color, and folded and rotated his shorts so one wouldn't wear out any faster than the other. A throwback to the days when his family had so little money.

Yet they had so much in common.

They loved retailing. The two worked at Abraham & Strauss in Brooklyn, the flagship store in a large chain on the East coast. They both started in the executive training squads and worked their way up; Allen becoming the Notions buyer and Terry a department manager in handbags. At home, at night, they talked shop. For decades, even after I came along and then my sister, Sam, that never stopped.

I showed up Sept. 27, 1972.

This was the same month that *The Waltons* started on television. What did I have in common with John-boy? What did my family have in common with the Waltons? Nothing whatsoever.

By the time I arrived, my parents had moved to St. Louis and were two years into a business they started on Forsyth Boulevard in Clayton; a small bookstore called The Library, Ltd. It was very limited, just a small space. They felt the venture was a risk worth taking. The store was well situated across the street from a Famous-Barr department store, a mile from Washington University. The community was and still is populated with scholars and business people. My mom and dad hired an architect to design their store and make it classy. They carved a children's book section out of a store room, and hung framed prints of Chagall, Mondrian and Matisse on the walls above the books.

Those early days were tough and unbusy. Dad would doze at the cash register. My grandma, Selma, would stand outside the store and fix her gaze on passers-by until she arrested their attention and got them to look at the store. She willed them in. Often the day's receipts would total less than $50.

By the fall of '72 when I was born, the store had gotten very busy. My dad was always bringing work home for my mom to do in her spare time. Seven years later when my sister Samantha came along, she was born on a Tuesday and my mom was back at work on Friday. My grandma was incredulous, "Why didn't you just have the baby in a field?" she exclaimed.

You could hardly call either of my parents neglectful; my mom found wonderful housekeepers/nannies who took great care of us. She was home at 5 p.m. for dinner most nights, and showed up for all our school functions.

One of the things I looked forward to every year was going to Sea Island, an idyllic resort off the coast of Georgia. Sea Island was at the same time luxurious and very down to earth. The kindest people live there; a land where they never tell you no. My sister and I loved to swim, hang out at the beach, play tennis and run around with the junior counselors. We would ride horses on the beach, watch the dolphins play in the ocean, and appreciate how small we were and how big and beautiful the world was. Sea Island was so magical that when the time came, I insisted on getting married there. The Sea Island colors, pink and green, are incorporated into the logo of my real estate company. Those colors represent that island and the magic I experienced while there as a child. To this day, it remains my favorite place to vacation. Heaven on earth.

I knew my parents loved Sea Island as much as we did, and loved their business and couldn't wait to get back to their store. The Library, Ltd. was their fair-haired child. Samantha seemed to take this all in stride, but I was a bit more of a drama queen, and would lay a guilt trip on my parents. I often told my friends who had stay-at-home moms that I was adopted.

When the conversation at our dinner table would invariably take a left-turn away from me and on to business, I'd yelp, "Can't you people talk about anything but business?"

I attended Community School, a very well respected private school. I did not do well in class, nor with many of the kids who could tell I was just a little too different. I suffered from dyslexia, undiagnosed until fifth grade, so I was constantly playing catch-up. I nearly got kicked out of school in fifth grade after stealing the answer book in math from the teacher's desk.

I wasn't entirely clueless, and I had several great teachers who saw something in me and did a lot to help me adjust. Because of their efforts, I was able to overcome my terrible reading comprehension challenges and learn how to play well with others.

Still, I had to keep on doing that different drummer thing. When I was 13, I took my dad's car and went joy riding with my friends. I can hardly remember a day in middle school when I wasn't grounded.

Not long after that joy ride, my parents called me into the living room for a talk.

I have to tell you, at that time I was afraid of my dad, and quite honestly still am to this day. I knew that he loved me, adored me really, and he certainly never hit me. He would yell in a way that made it feel as if the walls were going to come tumbling down around me.

This time he spoke to me evenly, which was profoundly scary.

"We're thinking of sending you to boarding school if you don't straighten out," he said.

I was unaware of it at the time, but my parents weren't blaming me. They were quietly reproaching themselves. They thought they had failed me and the store had come between us.

At the time, I would have agreed. In many ways it was the store, my parents' love for their business, and their determination for success that shaped me, provided me with the passion and the drive to make something of myself.

It wasn't as if I hated the store. As a little kid, I used to love it when my mom presided over story hour in the children's section, reading a book aloud. Sometimes I would read to the kids, too. Though I was hampered to a degree by my dyslexia, it didn't stop me. I had most of the stories memorized and would simply know when to turn the pages at the right time. I was also clever enough to know that my job wasn't through when the story was over; I then made sure the kids' parents bought the book that I had just read. I had to close the sale just like my mom did.

Oh, was she ever great at that. To my mom, visitors to the store weren't customers, they were individuals with passions and interests. She would ask, "What have you read lately that you enjoyed?" She started where they started, whether they liked trashy fiction, self-help, or something high-tone.

She would walk customers over to a section, hand them a book, let them take ownership, then tell them about it. She would, of course, have already read the book and others by that author and others in the genre;

she could tell these customers exactly how much they were going to love this volume. "Never recommend a book you don't like even if you have 100 copies sitting on the shelf," she would say. "Your customer will remember and no longer trust you."

My mom taught me how to sell in an authentic and loving way, not ever once by telling how, but by showing me how, day after day at the store. I got my work ethic, approach to business and concern for clients through osmosis. It was burned into my soul.

As it turned out, my parents didn't send me away. I straightened up, at least a little bit. By then we had moved to a home in Clayton, a fairly posh suburb bordering St. Louis. We lived a stone's throw from beautiful Forest Park, and I attended Clayton High School, which arguably is one of the best high schools in the country. By then I had gotten on top of my learning issues and was doing pretty well in class. I was also getting good at making friends. I had a posse.

Still, I managed to get into a little bit of trouble. There was that day I didn't really feel like going to school, and as an excuse I told my Spanish teacher my grandmother had died. Well, wouldn't you know my teacher ran into my mom at that damn bookstore, and expressed her condolences. My grandma had died many years earlier.

Grounded. Again.

It may seem odd, but from these challenges came seeds of entrepreneurial success.

Really, who hasn't skipped out on class a time or two? I was actually almost a model citizen. With the help of Nick Otten, one of the great teachers at Clayton High, I helped start a community service club. I was among the first five in the club, and by the time we were finished, we had 150 members engaged in all sorts of projects. The satisfaction for me was helping those in need, building an organization from the ground up, and involving people in the act of giving back.

At Clayton High one year, we fell $1,200 short of our goal for homecoming. It didn't seem like a problem to me, so I picked up the phone, called 12 of my friends' parents and asked them each for $100. No big deal, problem solved.

Though I probably didn't recognize it at the time, my interest had been stoked by my grandma, Selma. She served as a volunteer at Jewish Hospital. I used to tag along with her all the time as a little girl and had set my sights on someday being a candy striper, a kind of a junior nurse, who wore red and white-striped pinafores.

By this time in the early 90s, I was working part-time at the bookstore. Inspired by my experience with Mr. Otten, I developed a community service project for the staff. I suggested to my parents that we set up a program allowing the staff two paid days off a month to do volunteer work in the community. I ran the program and kept track of who was doing what and when, and it worked quite nicely. These days you hear about such programs at companies nationwide. We were doing it at The Library, Ltd. way before it became popular.

I'd like to say that all of the experiences that shaped me as a businesswoman and entrepreneur were positive, but I can't. A stockbroker named Harry taught me a lot, but not in a good way. Harry officed in a building across the street from my parents' store. He needed someone to make cold calls to get people interested in the financial services and products that he offered. I was up for that. Harry put me in a storage room with stacks of papers and dirty boxes and gave me a list of people to call. What fun, sitting alone in a dirty room talking to people about what they should do with their money. Keep in mind, I'm 16 years old and a complete germaphobe, so this "office space" really grossed me out.

Strangely, they listened. I converted many cold calls into customers for Harry. Was he appreciative? Nope. No raise. No bonus. No kind words.

After several months, I quit. Of course, that got his attention. He called my dad and tried to get him to talk me into coming back. My dad asked a few pertinent questions like whether he ever gave me a raise, or a bonus, or a warm and fuzzy. When Harry said he had not, my dad told him to take a hike.

My dad is a tough hombre, but he was incredibly loyal to his staff members. The Library, Ltd. provided good pay and generous benefits, including full health and disability coverage (my dad remembered how his grandpa Sam fought for benefits on behalf of the hand launderers).

Lots of companies provide decent benefits. How many top officers at these companies go holiday shopping every year, buying gifts for the staff, not in bulk, but with an eye on a particular item that would delight a particular employee? My mom insisted on making time to do all of the shopping for their employees. They treated their staff members like family. So do I.

I'm so proud of the family I have come from; hardworking, smart, driven, loving, caring entrepreneurs, and truly dedicated to the communities in which they live.

2

Going Hollywood and Coming Home

My parents gave me lots of bricks to start building my foundation; the examples they set, their work ethic, their wisdom, their advice, and some financial support along the way. In the early part of my adulthood, I was spontaneous and liked adventure. I moved from St. Louis to Chicago, back to St. Louis, to Los Angeles, to Australia, back to Los Angeles, and finally back to St. Louis. You could say I sowed my wild oats.

After high school, I attended Lake Forest College outside of Chicago. I loved being near the big city and spent a lot of time there with friends. I was enchanted with the hustle and bustle of 7.5 million people among skyscrapers and in densely populated diverse neighborhoods. I found human dramas playing out all over town. I was starting to understand that the possibilities in life were endless, and my dreams and vision started forming rapidly. My intensity to apply the business principles that I had learned from my family was starting to come alive. I was 18 years old.

The students at Lake Forest were what I called "richies." Many came from prep schools on the East coast who couldn't get into the Ivys; not especially my type. The kids I ran with in Chicago were more "regular people". I went between studying at Lake Forest up the North shore, to heading 45 miles south to hang out in the city. Although I loved Chicago, I didn't love Lake Forest. It was so cold the entire second semester that I knew I couldn't get through another winter in Chicago.

My parents' business was expanding, and the experience that I could get from that expansion was monumental. Returning to St. Louis was a no-brainer for me. I could be involved in large events at the store that included authors like Anne Rice, Jay Leno, Martha Stewart, Colin Powell, Gloria Steinem, Hillary Clinton, and Bill Bradley.

Being a part of these events was invigorating. It was not about meeting the celebrities, it was the thrill of the success my parents were enjoying and the hard work and planning that goes into running a successful business.

Coming back to St. Louis was exactly what I wanted to do. I got my degree at Maryville University; I majored in political science with a minor in psychology. Just like my mom, I went away for my first year and came back to St. Louis to finish my degree.

Then it was time to make a living. I worked for the family business, and I wanted to have fun too. I could multi-task. By this time, the mid-1990s, I was into the band scene. My friends in St. Louis loved to go out at night and catch the latest acts. I managed a band called Freeze the Hopper, led by singer/songwriter Steve Shaw. Think Beatles White Album, Tom Petty and Wilco. I helped promote their CD, *Illusions of Grandeur*, and figured I'd ride to the top right along with Steve and his band.

Of course, you could only go so far in the entertainment business in St. Louis. When my parents sold their business and decided to move to Los Angeles, I moved as well. I was attached to my family at the hip and would hate not living in the same city. In addition, I loved the entertainment industry.

At my last show with Freeze the Hopper, an Australian band, Eddie Would Go, which has now morphed into The Go Set, an international band, opened for them and I had a life changing experience. I met people that were so different than anyone I had ever known. Just weeks after I moved to Los Angeles, Justin, from Eddie Would Go, invited me to go to Australia. I planned on going for three weeks, but ended up staying six months.

The people I met were astonishing. I could not get enough. Everyone in my world had always been so business focused, and the culture in Australia featured incredibly laid back, spontaneous, "you only live once" type of personalities. They spent the majority of their time outside, which was so different than my experiences. Having the capacity to work hard, and having that be only one segment of your life rather than the entire picture, is a lesson that I strive to embody and continue to struggle with to this day.

Funny thing, my parents did not have a conniption fit over this. You will remember my mom headed off for England after her college years. She just figured I would find my way. "Was it the wisest thing to do?" my mom would say in looking back. "Maybe not. Yes, a long term job would be nice. I didn't fit into what my parents thought my life should look like, so I wasn't real hysterical about what Kelly was doing."

After about six months of an unbelievable experience in Australia, I came back to Los Angeles where I worked for a great friend of mine, Sarah, a casting director. I worked on the movie *Hanging Up*, with Diane Keaton, Meg Ryan, Walter Matthau and Nora Efron.

One of my fondest memories when making the movie was when this 180-pound Newfoundland came in with his trainer. The dog was so well trained that when his handler threw out a 12" x 12" piece of wood and told the dog to stand on it, this enormous dog was able to get all four paws on that small piece of wood. The next part of the show we could have never imagined. In the movie, the dog was supposed to jump up on Diane Keaton. She didn't realize how big and strong the dog was, and went crashing down as he jumped on her. The entire office came flying to her rescue. The dog was devastated and just stood over her, licking her face. He was so sorry he had knocked her down. Needless to say, it was a very fun project.

Who would have ever thought I would have had the opportunity to be running around Australia with a rock band or working on movies? You never know where life is going to take you.

Funny, if my parents did get hysterical, then maybe I would have had something to push back against and kept on going to the wild side. Something was tugging me back to St. Louis. I didn't see a future in LA. Maybe, if I played my cards right, I'd be an assistant to a muckety-muck agent. I could also see how easy it would be to slip into the role of party girl. Something was telling me that I ought to find a day job with benefits, get married, have a family like boring, regular people. I wanted simple.

So I returned to St. Louis, chucked my exciting life in Los Angeles, and got into sales with Verizon. Remember the kid who at 16 was successful at cold calling? I had no fear of failure, I knew I could be successful. I started as a temp, became a business account executive and then a major account manager within 18 months. I worked really hard, learned a lot about long term sales, and how to communicate with all kinds of people. Constant communication was extremely important. Some of my biggest accounts have become great friends. Trust was being built on a personal as well as business level. Verizon is where I increased my knowledge in dealing with large, corporate clients. People are people, and relatability, along with communication, collaboration and drive, equals success.

While at Verizon, I was invited to one of my client's Christmas parties. I was the only vendor invited to attend as I had developed such great rapport. That's where I met Brian, my husband to be, and just the kind of man I was looking for. He was good looking, easy going, and hard working. Brian grew up on a farm, and people used to tease us that we were like the couple from the

TV show *Green Acres*; he loved the farm and I loved the Ritz Carlton. We bought a home in the burbs, brought two very large, affectionate dogs, Bodi, a Lab, and Clyde, a Great Dane, into our lives, and started trying to make a baby.

Meanwhile at Verizon, one of the higher-ups noticed my work and took me with him to MCI, another telecommunications giant. He put me in charge of a staff of 18 across St. Louis, southern Illinois, and Kansas City.

I had, at that time, no management training and my dad's personality; how do you think that worked out? I micromanaged and then compensated by stepping in for my staff and doing everything myself. Not proud of this, but at the time I would think to myself, if those dumb shits would work 10 percent harder, they could make so much more money and so could I.

I went back into sales, much to my relief, and I am sure to the relief of those I had been supervising.

Pharmaceutical sales was an interesting and lucrative field. So I quit my job at MCI to take a job in the pharmaceutical world, not realizing I had to pass all of these exams with a 90 percent to keep my job. Remember, I have dyslexia.

Still, I was smart enough to compensate for it and

passed. Many people didn't make it through and were sent home. I had a month of training at home, and then got shipped off to Texas for three weeks, bound in a hotel, studying morning, noon, and night so that I could speak to cardiologists about treating their patients. It was a challenge, and I like to be challenged.

I learned so much about marketing while working in the pharmaceutical world. It seemed odd and unsatisfying to me though, calling on the same doctors over and over and over again, giving them the same bits of information, lunch and samples week after week. I came to understand that I am a driver. I need a beginning, middle, and end in the sales process. Although I learned a ton, I was not satisfied in this role.

As I mentioned earlier, after getting married, Brian and I were trying to make a baby. Brady was born January 28, 2007. It was the best day of my life. Who knew how much life would change? All of a sudden I was responsible for someone other than myself, and I loved it. The love you feel for your child is different than any other love you can experience. I worked from home so I could spend as much time with Brady during the day as possible.

As you will recall, my mom didn't stop working when she had us. Neither did I. I had moved from pharmaceutical sales into real estate, a venture that suited me to a T as I will explain later. I didn't stop there. I chaired my neighborhood social committee, organizing the Halloween parade and weenie roast, the Christmas celebration that included pictures with Santa, carriage rides and tons of food, the Easter egg hunt, and the summer picnic with pony rides. Even that wasn't enough to fill me up. I started an organization called Neighbors Helping Neighbors, that helps disadvantaged families with basic needs. We started with a family that included a nine-year-old girl who had been sleeping on the floor, not having a bed of her own since she was an infant. Of course, we provided the bed and more, and then kept looking for more families to help. We were up to more than a dozen within a year.

I was Supermom, Supercitizen, Supersaleswoman. Little did I know that I was heading for a fall.

3

Hell Bent, Headed for a Fall

Fake it till you make it.

You've heard many people use that expression. I first heard it from the number one agent in my city who was with the firm I had just joined.

I had gotten my real estate license, but had yet to make a sale. What she said to me and other agents at an open house made an impression on me. You may not be sure of yourself, but then no one has to know that. You may not know everything, but then you can always quietly bust your butt to find out. Faking it doesn't mean you are putting anything over on anyone, it simply means that you are substituting confidence for fear.

Clients want to believe it's all going to go well when they are buying or selling a home. So I had to give them someone to believe in. Me.

How could I possibly pull this off with hardly any real estate experience? Easy. I tapped into what my parents had taught me. As you have read earlier, my mom sold books, not simply by knowing what was inside the volume but knowing what was inside the head of the would-be reader. She connected with them on a personal level. If the customers trusted my mom, they would likely buy the book just on her say so; more importantly, they would come back and buy many more.

My dad had a gift for seeing over the horizon. Today we call that vision. He had big ideas and he had no doubt that he would accomplish them. That assurance came from winning in cards and winning in business. He not only was supremely confident, he was super competitive. He kept an eye on what everyone was doing around him and upped the ante. No one would outwork him and no one could outsmart him. If you worked for my mom and dad, as I did, you too, had better work hard and work smart. I did.

Chelsea and Matt were my first clients. Of course, at the time they didn't know that minor detail. I was Kelly, the savvy real estate agent, who was going to put them in a great home. I was also Kelly, their new best friend.

We did things together beyond buying a house. Chelsea and I went to lunch. They had a two-year-old daughter, so I introduced Chelsea to my friends who had children that age. I would arrange play dates and we would all go to the park to talk and hang out.

It wasn't until recently that I mentioned to Chelsea, "You know, you were my first client."

"No way," she said. "You knew everything!"

This all happened nearly ten years ago, but Chelsea remembers to this day what I did that really impressed her. We were standing outside a house she liked in a very pleasant neighborhood when Chelsea expressed her concerns. The neighborhood looked great; the home was wonderful, but who lived in this neighborhood? Were there kids the same age as her daughter that she could play with and be friends with at school?

I could have said, "Well, of course." Maybe I could have pointed to a swing set or a basketball court in someone's backyard.

Instead, I went next door, knocked on the door, introduced myself and Chelsea, and asked the neighbor if she would talk about what life was like in her subdivision. What she said was reassuring. Of course, she could have said any number of things that might have turned Chelsea away. That would have been just fine because the whole idea is not to get a contract, but to put Chelsea and her family in the kind of place they would want to raise their children.

They are still living in the home that she and Matt purchased those many years ago. They now have two children, having added a son, now age 7, the same age as my son, Brady. They come to my neighborhood for holiday events and are big supporters of our charitable causes.

So I didn't just make a sale, I made a friend. That friend has referred several other clients to me. They too, are now my friends.

I tell my staff that you have to love on your clients in any way that you can. Some of them are very hard to love, at least at first. That makes me think of Jack and Jill (not real names of course). At first, Jack acted like a complete jerk. "I might buy a house today. I might buy a house six months from today. I don't know when I'm going to buy a house. Does that scare you?"

I simply said, "I want you to find the house that makes the most sense for you and your family. If that means we find it today, that's great."

He said, "Well we're not going to. It's going to take us six months."

I said, "That's okay." Why? Because the most important thing you can do beyond projecting confidence in who you are, is putting your clients' fears to rest. Jack's fear was that he was going to be railroaded by an overzealous agent.

I spent the whole day with Jack and Jill, building trust as we went from one house to the next. I continued to let them know that it hardly mattered if they signed a contract sooner or later.

Turned out it was sooner. In fact, that day. Late in the afternoon, they walked into a home with a superb kitchen and well within their price range.

"What are the odds that I'm going to find another house with a kitchen this nice at this price?" Jack asked me.

"About five percent," I said matter-of-factly. By then, because I had persuaded Jack that I was in no hurry, he knew he could trust my advice, and he could trust me.

"Let's do this," Jack said.

———

The home buying and selling process is so emotional. Real estate agents never tell, but you find yourself in some precarious situations. Whether people are getting married, divorced, having babies, etc., you are moving them to the next chapter of their lives. It's a privilege, and it takes a tender heart, caring soul, and great negotiation skills.

Just as your client has to have confidence in you, you have to have confidence in the brokerage house with which you are affiliated. I've met great brokers and mentors in real estate over the years, and some not so great. The important part to remember is you learn from both.

Generally speaking, the difference is in whether brokers care about you as a human being. If they do, they understand who you are, where you are coming from and what you need to get better. If they don't, you'll know it. Each encounter with them is a transaction.

I went from about a year with Coldwell Banker Gundaker, to about 2 years with RE/MAX, to 5½ years at Keller Williams, where I was a partner in the ownership group. All three experiences had their good and bad. The most important piece in all three was the wonderful people I met. I learned to write a contract, negotiate the deal, close the contract, and have happy clients. I also came to understand how to work with the other 24 people who are also part of a real estate transaction. Hire the right team members, build a team and build a sustainable business.

At Keller Williams I had several amazing mentors. The biggest influencer was, and still is today, my friend Matt. We became close friends when we reviewed my personality assessment. We immediately understood each other having both come from entrepreneurial families that started with very little and built successful corporations. We discovered that growing up we actually only lived 10 minutes apart. Matt was my partner in one of the Keller Williams franchises, and is one of the savviest people I know. Not only is he smart, he is a tremendous asset to those he gives his attention. Although he's moved a couple of times to different cities since we've known each other, we still communicate frequently and visit each other. I often seek his advice and guidance. His knowledge of the business landscape is phenomenal, and if I were stuck on the side of the road, he's one of those "go to" guys you know you can depend on. I've never met anyone else like him or his amazing family.

There were a couple of regional directors who really taught me how to build a team. I hold these people in such high regard, for without that knowledge I wouldn't be where I am today.

I was given the honor of speaking at several of the Keller Williams national conventions. It was so much fun to speak to an audience of 8,000 people! If you would have asked me five years ago if I would have ever done something like that, I would have told you no way. It was such a rewarding experience to give back and share my knowledge, just as my mentors had done for me.

During my time at Keller Williams, I received the Cultural Icon Award three years in a row. This is a national award that is given to a very select group of people who love to give back to the culture and community surrounding them. Giving back in this community was really fun because I had learned so much.

As I mentioned earlier, I learned from Keller Williams how to build a collaborative team. Fortunately, by then I had already met the person who would become one of my most important teammates, Tracy Kirkpatrick.

She will be the first of many compadres that I will tell you about. Each will have a turn telling you, through their eyes, about this journey that we have taken. They all love me, of course! You may be surprised how candid they will be about my faults. For instance, Tracy came this close to leaving me and yet now we are joined at the hip.

How did that happen?

Well, I will let her tell the story.

It's Easter time, 2006 and my husband Joe comes in the door and says, "Hey, I'm going to Kelly Hager's house tonight and we're all going to stuff Easter eggs for the neighborhood Easter event."

That got my attention. "WHO got YOU to stuff Easter eggs?" Understand that my husband is a big, burly, general contractor who doesn't take orders well from anyone (kind of a tough guy). The last thing I would ever expect him to do is stuff Easter eggs.

"Kelly Hager, and she said she really needs my help, and there's going to be drinks and appetizers, so I'm going."

Kelly had gotten Joe's attention for another reason. He was gutting and rehabbing a home in Lake Saint Louis and looking to flip it. He told me that Kelly Hager was this big real estate agent in our neighborhood, and he wanted her to sell this house for us. We went to dinner with Kelly and her husband, and she had this really long listing presentation. I liked her right off the bat, she had an incredible energy. I told her it was fine to list the house, Joe believed in her and that was good with me. I finally got her to stop talking about the listing presentation so we could enjoy dinner!

Kelly then listed our house and she got it under contract quickly. I didn't find out until I started working for her that following year and began tracking her sales, that our Lake Saint Louis house was the biggest listing that she had to that point. Here I thought she was this million-dollar baller (kind of speaks to the "fake it until you make it" philosophy).

I couldn't help but be attracted to Kelly's can-do spirit. She was both likeable and irrepressible. I knew she was going to be a big success, though at the time she had just 18 months in the real estate business.

Kelly was growing her business, and was in need of some help. She had the vision and the work ethic, but someone had to take care of the nuts and bolts, as she just didn't have the time. She asked me if I would join her, and the timing was right. I had recently taken an early retirement from AT&T where I had been a performance manager in its call center. I wanted something flexible, so I could pick my daughter up from school. Kelly says, 'Oh yeah...you can work whenever you want. That's fine.' Sounded great to me!

Kelly says, "Do you have any questions?"

"No, not really," I said. And I'm thinking, "How hard could this be?"

She wanted me to start right away ... during the holidays. I said no, we were taking a family vacation. That may have been the only time ... at least for quite awhile, that Kelly took no for answer.

I started with Kelly at RE/MAX, where we were in an office so small we couldn't scoot our chairs out from our desks at the same time. Three weeks later, her son Brady was born and she moved her office, and me, to her home so she could spend more time with Brady.

Kelly was raised by nannies, as her mother and father were workaholics. She also had a nanny to care for Brady, and it was a good thing because she, too, was a workaholic. The apple doesn't fall far from the tree.

Those first few years she went through quite a few nannies, as none compared to Freddie, who was her favorite nanny growing up. Freddie was Kelly's second mother, and she keeps in touch with her to this day. She picked her up from school every day, helped her with homework, ran her around to all of her activities, and cooked dinner for the family. Freddie also stayed with Kelly and her sister Samantha when their parents traveled. All nannies that came through the door were always compared to Freddie. It was so odd to me, as my mom stayed home with me in my younger years. I had friends whose moms worked, but none that had nannies; such a foreign concept to me.

I would get to her house at 8 a.m. each day, and she would be sitting there already at work in her T-shirt and underwear. She was so passionate to start her day that she wouldn't take time to get dressed before heading downstairs to her home office. I'd say… "Couldn't you at least put on some pants before you get too involved in the day?" I was horrified that a client would stop by and find her this way… and it happened. We had to hide her from room to room to get her to her closet without being seen! One of the many escapades/challenges in dealing with Kelly.

She would give me stuff to do and then totally double-check everything. It wasn't that she didn't appreciate what I was doing, she just thought nobody could do it as well as she could.

Oh, was she demanding.

"Have you got that ready?" she'd say.

"Kelly, you just gave it to me."

"I have got to be out the door!"

I am a very hard worker, but Kelly ... she was hell bent.

It's Friday afternoon, 5:50 (and I normally worked until 6:00). I am preparing to leave to get a start on the weekend with my family and Kelly would say, "You know before you leave, we could get started on this or that." She never wanted to feel like she was being taken advantage of.

"Really, Kelly, it's ten to six," I would be thinking, but of course would never say that aloud.

She would get this look of disgust on her face like I was abandoning her.

Kelly could just never seem to relax and have fun, and if she did do something fun, it was purposeful with a business agenda in the background. If she had a dinner party, all of the guests were clients or vendors. Never just a group of friends to hang out. She was always "on."

By 2010, the stress from her intensity was just getting to be too much for me. I told my husband that life is too short, I really didn't feel like I wanted to be in this position much longer.

Then Kelly got sick. The world changed for her, for me, for so many people in her circle. It got much worse... and then so much better....

4

People Who Surround You Matter

We called my illness my summer nap.

Maybe I needed one. As you can tell from Tracy's account, I was working, working, working, and driving everyone around me crazy.

You don't have to take Tracy's word for it. Talk to my friend Chandra. I met Chandra in 2002 when she moved to St. Louis from Chicago. She was working as a cosmetologist at a spa that I frequented.

Chandra didn't know many people in St. Louis at the time, and as I often do, I just kind of adopted her and helped her find her way in St. Louis. She was really smart and very determined, and loved to stir the pot; my kind of girl. We quickly became great friends.

This was not a one-way street. Before Tracy came on board, Chandra would help me in my real estate business. She'd help me organize the Easter egg hunt in our subdivision, the fall festivals, Christmas events, cookie baking for our clients, and worked on the Adopt-A-Family program. When I was trying to get pregnant and going through an in vitro fertilization process, it was Chandra who gave me the shots in the butt every day. She's like a sister to me.

Chandra is a candid friend. We grew up very differently, yet share so many of the same values. She was a college athlete growing up in Chicago, and is one of the most competitive people I know. Our families are connected at the hip. "Go big or go home, right?" we would both say.

Strong women surround me, from Tracy, to Chandra, to Jamie. Jamie is a bit of a workaholic just like me, another sister. Jamie worked out of the Keller Williams office arranging mortgage loans, and we loved to talk shop about how we would grow our businesses.

After I put Brady in bed, I'd text Jamie, "Are you ready?" Then I'd dial her up and we'd talk sometimes past midnight. We were growing our brands together. I guess we would both be classified as die-hards. We both made time for family, but the majority of our time was spent on building business and teams. It's a drive and a passion that is uncontrollable, and it's a blessing and a curse all wrapped into one.

It's not that I ran off from my family and spent all my time at work. When Brady came along I set up my house so I could work from home and be with him. I could never put work out of my mind, and I was careening from one supersized project to the next. Many were successful, which only encouraged me to do more.

Then one day, July 1, 2010, it all began to unravel. That evening I didn't feel well, it was very strange. The best way I can describe it was almost like an out-of-body experience. I had bronchitis a few weeks before and I thought maybe it was trying a comeback.

"Why don't you take an Advil and see how you feel in the morning?" Brian said.

By 5 a.m. I felt worse. Still Brian wondered if it could really be that bad. "I am telling you there is something terribly wrong," I said. "You've got to get me to the hospital." I felt so odd, very weird feeling. My body had never felt like this before. Other than an emergency room visit for a sprained ankle, I had never been in a hospital. We drove to Progress West Hospital, just 10 minutes away. On the way, I called my mom, and she immediately flew in from Los Angeles.

The medics could easily see that I was in trouble. My blood pressure had spiked, something like 212/148.

That's stroke territory. I was vomiting. Yet they couldn't determine what was wrong with me. It took the doctors more than a week to get me stable enough to send me home.

I was home for a period of time, and was not getting any better; quite the opposite. I was vomiting uncontrollably, getting completely dehydrated and worse by the moment. I went back to Progress West, where I was admitted for a second time. Infectious disease doctors, kidney specialists, neurologists, and every other specialist at that hospital came and went trying to figure out what was wrong. I was still vomiting day and night. The dehydration caused me to become delirious, and I had lost most of my strength. My capacity for conversation was dwindling. Everyone was panicked; frustration and fear were setting in, not only for me but for those around me. I kept thinking, "what in the hell can this possibly be?" Nobody knew the answer. Very mysterious.

Can you imagine what was going through the minds of my mother and father, and my close circle of friends? The doctors were running out of tests to give and still no answers. I still wasn't getting any better, in fact just the opposite. Curiosity, confusion, frustration and helplessness were the emotions running through everyone.

After another week of treating symptoms at Progress West, I was homeward bound. They were hoping the medication adjustments made to treat my symptoms while I was in the hospital would do the trick; they didn't. I was home for a short amount of time, getting worse by the day.

While back at home, I asked my dad one evening, "Where is the bathroom?" Keep in mind I lived in this house for 10 years, and the bathroom was 10 feet away from where I was sitting. I got up, walked into the wall, and fell. My dad immediately took me back to the hospital. This time we went to Missouri Baptist as the first hospital had run out of ideas.

The testing continued....every test available, including MRI's, spinal taps, blood work every five minutes (or so it seemed), full body scans, liver biopsy, ultrasounds, etc. I became incoherent at this point and had to be restrained. I was moving around and so agitated that I had pulled out all of my tubes. I had no idea what was happening. The doctors told my family it was due to my enzymes being so out of balance.

As I'm sharing this part of my life, you may think I seem somewhat detached and unemotional. Keep in mind, I was first incoherent and then in a coma, on life support, with my organs shutting down, and not only did I not know what was going on around me, I really have no memory of the majority of this time. It almost feels to me like I'm telling you a very sad story about someone else's life.

After a few weeks in this hospital, most of which was spent in the intensive care unit, completely incoherent, they were still unable to diagnose what was wrong with me. They could tell my family everything I didn't have, but not what I did. Weird. I was getting worse by the hour, so I was then transferred via ambulance to the world renowned teaching hospital in town, Barnes-Jewish, to see if doctors there could figure it out.

After arriving at Barnes, I was immediately put into a medically induced coma and on life support; my organs were shutting down and survival was the underdog. The doctors were trying everything, every test known to man, different medicines, my blood work was sent to the Mayo Clinic; my parents were scared to death. No one was in or out; my mom would speak to a couple of people daily to spread the word.

My parents were told a second time that I might die, or when I came to, I might be a vegetable. When I did wake up, my brain capacity was not available. I had little memory and I could barely stay awake for weeks. I had no strength, I could not walk, I could not see because my double vision was so bad, I could not open both of my eyes at the same time. My communication was almost nil. How could this be happening? How could three hospitals with the best doctors not figure out what was going on? In any case, I would never be the same.

And that was very much the case.

———

As you will recall, Tracy Kirkpatrick, my assistant, was about to leave me when I got sick. She loved me. I loved her. Tracy decided she could no longer deal with my micromanaging and my non-stop obsession with work.

Had I known what Tracy had in mind, I would have been very upset. For a while, I might have even felt betrayed. Ultimately I would have understood and moved on. We would still be friends.

That's not what happened. When I fell ill, Tracy not only stayed, she stepped up.

I'll let her describe what happened next.

When Kelly got sick, I figured she was going to be out for a week or so. Not a big deal. I jumped into her calendar and rescheduled all of her appointments. That took a ton of phones calls and lots of time as Kelly always had her calendar booked from sun up until sun down. Then a week passed and she was no better. Actually worse. Then we are into week three.

I remember that her dad called me aside at that point and asked with a great deal of concern: "Are we in danger of you leaving?"

"No, of course not," I said. "I would never do that. I just wouldn't."

By this time, there are five of us either working full or part-time with Kelly. We had moved from Kelly's home to the Keller Williams office. We had sales of $12-14 million annually and were quite busy. Kelly was the face of this business and increasingly we were getting calls from people who wanted to see only Kelly. We really tried to downplay the seriousness of her illness, as we didn't want to alarm our clients and disrupt the business.

Of course, I had to take on that role. I did fine with most of the clients, but there was one client who had just ripped me a new one over some ridiculous issue. When Kelly was feeling a little better, I went to her asking how she wanted it handled.

Kelly said, "You should just fire him as a client. No one should have to put up with that." Well, I loved that she was so supportive of me, but I was thinking, this is NOT Kelly. She would have gone into detail about how to win over that client, telling me just what to say and what to do. I wanted to say to Kelly, "Who are you and what did you do with Kelly?"

Ultimately, I did fire that client, but couldn't believe I did so, and with her direction no less. In those days, we NEVER terminated a relationship with a client, even if that person was extremely unrealistic, rude, egotistical and just plain mean.

Then I remember talking with her about a sticky issue with a staff member. And Kelly said, "Do whatever you think is right." Again I'm thinking, who is this person? The way that Kelly was relying on me now was completely different than the way she had relied on me before.

Then Kelly added, "Look, it's 6 o'clock. You have a family. You should get on home."

What?

I got really scared at that point. I thought, something is seriously wrong with Kelly, more than they are telling us, for her to be talking this way. Those were words that would NEVER come out of her mouth.

Of course, we all ended up working many more hours on behalf of the business than we ever had before. We were learning as we went and we all felt like we knew the business so much better. The people at Keller Williams were great. They would bring in meals and want to do anything they could to support Kelly, her family and her staff. Kelly was such a giver at the office, teaching classes, mentoring peers and genuinely caring *about her KW family, that they were all anxious to do anything they could to help her.*

The hardest part was that everyone was so worried about Kelly. Sharon, a longtime friend of mine had just joined us as an agent. We would just cry over what was happening with Kelly first thing in the morning when we received updates from her family. Then we'd say, we have to quit talking about it and get to work. We asked the people at Keller Williams if we could just provide them a once a day update on Kelly and not have to respond to so many well-intentioned queries. Otherwise, we were never going to be able to focus. We would then close the door, close the blinds and get to work. I knew at this point that the business was resting on my shoulders, and that was not a comfortable position for me, yet it was a matter of survival.

When Kelly returned, at first part-time and at half speed, she could see that we had so many things well in hand. This was reassuring to her and I'm sure is part of what led to the person we call "New Kelly." New Kelly empowers us instead of micromanaging. New Kelly can step back and see the big picture, take some time for herself and her family and live in the moment instead of always plotting and planning the next big thing for the business. As difficult as she had been at times, we had grown used to working with Old Kelly. Now we had to adjust. In a short period of time, I had gone from doing exactly what Kelly said to do, to running the business in her absence. Now that Kelly was back and different, I had to be different as well.

––––––

Yes, everything was different. This was dawning on me as I came out of the coma and coming to grips with a new world.

After the first week of being awake and making small amounts of progress each day, my dad returned to Los Angeles to check on the houses and my mom took an overnight trip to Chicago to see my sister Samantha, who was 8 ½ months pregnant at the time.

My husband, knowing that I would be all alone, walked in my hospital room and told me he wanted a divorce, and then left.

All I could think about was, why is this happening now? I had just come out of a coma. Why did he make the decision at this point to ask for a divorce? Very troubling timing.

Just when I thought I had already hit bottom and life couldn't have gotten any worse, this news scared me to my incredibly weakened core. I was still in a wheelchair, unable to walk, couldn't see clearly, my brain power was severely diminished, and my memory was failing me continuously.

My son, at this point, was three years old. What was I going to do?

I faced months of rehabilitation, not knowing whether I would become reasonably ambulatory, regain my eye-hand coordination, or be able to put my thoughts together in a consistent and coherent manner. I could not get around at all. Driving was not an option, I couldn't see.

I had been pretty far gone, so far gone that my parents were thinking about how they would care for Brady. At one point they were asked to sign a DNR (Do Not Resuscitate directive), which they flatly refused.

My mother was doing everything she could to hold herself together, but was crumbling on the inside. Both she and my dad flew in from California, alternatively keeping a vigil at my bedside and seeing to Brady's needs. My mom did more than hold my hand, she was my advocate. As the doctors struggled to find out what was wrong with me, she did her own research. She asked questions and, at times when it was necessary, gave the nursing staff the "what for."

Though I pulled through and came out the better for

it, my mother, to this day, does not look on any of this as a growing experience. "I am not a better person for having gone through this. It was the worst time in my life," my mom said in looking back. "I was seeing my child lose ground every day and no one could give us solutions."

I think the worst time came when they took Kelly to rehabilitation where she was put in the same facility where my father had spent his last days in the nursing home side of the facility. They took Kelly in an ambulance and I followed in my car. When I arrived at the parking lot, I could not get out of the car. I must have stayed in the car for a half an hour weeping, until finally I said to myself, "Okay, get out of the car, put one foot in front of the other."

Then, I mustered up enough strength to tell myself that Kelly is going to get through this. I looked at it as a battle every single day. Kelly is going to get well. She is going to get out of here.

Where would I be without my mom? I simply don't know. Sometimes I was barely aware of what was going on around me and on my behalf. Sorry Mom, but looking back, some of what I went through was fairly hilarious.

Like the time I woke up in the middle of the night

at the hospital. I had just come out of the coma and realized for the first time that I had been hooked up to catheters front and rear. Uncomfortable to say the least. If you've never experienced this, I hope you never have to. I turned on the television and heard an ad for a waffle maker. It seemed perfectly logical to me that a waffle iron could be used to extract the catheters. Someone needed to know; hence, I called my Uncle Jerome, who is in the commercial real estate business and has a staff of workers handy with tools. If memory serves, it was about 4 a.m. Uncle Jerome picks up the phone and the first thing he hears is this: "You have to get your men down here and have them get this thing out of my ass." Of course, they would need the waffle iron to do the job.

The first time I saw Uncle Jerome after having left the hospital and rehabilitation facility was for dinner at one of our favorite restaurants. I came hobbling in on my walker with my mom at my side, and when I saw him, I had this flashback from the conversation about the catheters and the waffle iron. But surely, that must have been a dream.

I had to ask. The look on Uncle Jerome's face told me all that I needed to know. It had happened. The good news was that by then I was cognizant enough to feel embarrassed. This is how you measure progress.

5

Starting Over

As I grew stronger and better able to take care of myself, I began to think about going back to work. Matt, one of my partners and a mentor at Keller Williams, encouraged me to take it slowly. We both recognized that my team, led by Tracy at this point, had done an outstanding job. "Do not take one thing back," Matt said. "Everything you have given up, do not take one thing back."

That was easy advice to follow at first, as I didn't have the capacity to show property or go on listing appointments. Nor did I have the desire. Even using a walker, I could barely maneuver. I had very little strength, brain capacity or fire in my belly…it just wasn't there.

What was I going to do all day? I couldn't even handle daytime television. I am quite sure, even to this day, that *Three's Company* reruns are hazardous to your health. I had no idea how to move forward.

Matt told me to start by meeting with potential vendors. I didn't even know how to have a business conversation at that point. How would I be able to persuade someone to work with me? My "meeting" and "please work with me" skills had deteriorated tremendously. Still, I trusted Matt. He helped me through my darkest hours. He knew my behavior would mean little to people who wanted my business.

Another friend and business associate, who is affectionately nicknamed DC3, helped me in a different way. Through conversation and active listening over coffee, he opened a door to my spiritual side that had long been shut. As noted in my introduction, God didn't show up when my organs were shutting down, nor when they fired up again. No special messages.

I do believe God put me on a path, a path that requires me at times to stop and reflect. Everyone looks at spirituality in a different way. I close my eyes and thoughts run through my head that speak of hopes, not fears. I ask for peace and a way forward so that I can bring insight and learning first to myself, then to my son, Brady, and to the people around me. I have always wanted to be an encourager and I think about ways to do that effectively. I am thankful, I am appreciative, and I am grateful.

I cannot say God wasn't a part of my life before. I never gave my spiritual side much of an opening. I was focused on success without really knowing what that meant. In a sense, God did me a favor by afflicting me with an illness that didn't kill me, but slowed me down enough to reflect on who I was and where I was going. I guess God deserved a lot more credit than I ever gave to him.

This was part of New Kelly that my friends, family and colleagues were beginning to notice. Let me hasten to add, parts of Old Kelly remained—the Kelly with new ideas, the risk taker with that forever sense of urgency. It just took a while for those qualities to re-emerge. Gratitude also emerged. The loyalty and dedication of my team members, my friends, and my family was unbelievable. To this day, I can hardly comprehend what all of these people did on my behalf.

So what can I share with you that perhaps would put you on the right track, or if you are already there, keep you headed in the right direction? Create rules for happiness. Reflect on what makes you happy. Write them down and execute them.

My rules for happiness:

1. Do what I can to keep my family, friends and myself healthy.

2. Surround myself with the strongest, most amazing team so that business and opportunities are coming in daily.

3. Assure that my calendar is set for the week, fairly set for the next month, and structured for the next year. Schedule both personal time and business time. Follow my schedule to a T; this simplifies my life.

4. Travel.

5. Reconnect with people throughout my life.

6. Meet new people.

7. Strive for greatness daily with solution-based people.

8. Go the extra mile and make a difference in someone's life as much as possible.

9. Exercise.

10. Pursue financial freedom.

What are your rules for happiness?

All of this and a lot more takes commitment. Commitment can be viewed in many ways. If you are committed and dedicated to a cause, you do everything in your power to achieve the results that you seek. You are on a journey to get to the desired outcome. This can be business, this can be personal, but it is the teamwork that gets you through the journey.

I am dedicated to building a team of entrepreneurs that have drive, can collaborate with a sense of urgency, are loyal to each other, and are committed to great client service.

I won't elaborate on every one of the happiness rules listed above. Most are self-explanatory, but I do want to discuss reconnection and meeting new people.

I can't believe how many people have come back into my life in recent years. It's funny how people who you once trusted and were such a large part of your life, resurface out of nowhere. My friend Jeannette, who I first met when I was six years old and remained good friends with through high school, has recently come back into my life. Some of my great friends from Clayton High School have come back as well; many of my old friends have moved back to town. Even the girls from Camp Birchwood, where I spent my summers sailing as a teenager, have resurfaced. Who would have ever thought that one of my besties from Australia would pop back in after 16 years? How fun is that?

These people know me; the good, the bad, and the ugly, and there is such a deep level of trust. We have just picked up where we left off. My friends who know me from back in the day keep me centered and provide a perspective that you cannot always get from those with whom you work.

On the flip side, new found friends are both a delight and a necessity. When I woke up from the coma and came back home, I needed a full time nanny, not only for Brady, but for myself. I was so lucky that I found a friend and more in Kim.

I met Kim at one of my family's favorite restaurants. She was a hostess and a server, the kind of person who immediately made you comfortable and feel at home. She grew up in Chesterfield, not far from where The Kelly Hager Group has its office today. Her family ran a small business, an ice cream franchise, and like me she had grown up watching her parents struggle and succeed. As Kim remembered, her mom and dad never really took a day off. "It would be Christmas and there was mom crunching numbers," she recalled. Along with her schooling, Kim had been working five days a week since she was 14.

Kim joined me in early 2011 to help take care of Brady

and to act as a personal assistant. She found me to be nothing like what her friends who had known me from years before had told her. At the time I was vulnerable, low key, skittish, and still needed a lot of help.

"Kelly couldn't walk up stairs, her son had to move to the first level of the house," she remembered. "She couldn't walk on a patterned carpet because it was so disorienting."

There were so many limitations in my brain that had to be relearned, almost as if I was a baby. I didn't need the annoying *Super Nanny*, which was a popular show at the time. Nor perhaps did I need someone who knew me from before and might grow impatient with my halting progress.

In the early going, Kim was a far greater help to me than I could be for her. Yes, that patterned carpet was throwing me, along with lots of other things, and Kim was there to help me navigate and anticipate all my needs.

You could say she was the answer to my prayers. As noted, one of my prayers was to be an encourager, to shine a light on a path forward for other people. One of the things that makes me proud and gives me hope is that as I grew stronger and built my business, it created a place for someone like Kim to step up and succeed.

As Brady got older and spent more time in school, and I got stronger, Kim would come into our office to help with the business. Curious and proactive by nature, Kim jumped into learning all she could about real estate. She got her real estate license and has taken on the role of marketing coordinator.

As I regained my footing and dove back into the business in a different way, Kim joined with the others in accommodating New Kelly. Her perspective is interesting because in it you will see measures of both appreciation and apprehension concerning how I work.

Said Kim:

Before I joined KHG, I didn't like to take too many risks. I wanted to know my next step before I took it. Kelly's approach was, "Here's the outcome I want. I don't know exactly the next steps we need to take yet, but we're going to do it.

That would leave many of us scared. Uh, oh, she's really reaching again. There's a reason that our company is doing so well, that the team has quadrupled in the last four years. Kelly reaches high. She keeps saying this is "going to happen," even if it looks scary or impossible. That keeps us motivated.

Now I'm not so scared about dreaming and setting big goals. I learned to stop asking myself, "How are we going to do that?" when Kelly has a new or updated strategy. I believe that together we will figure it out.

One way to be successful, Kelly has taught me, is to write it down. Don't just think it, or say it, write it down. Kelly writes down her goals and she keeps looking at them. The other thing she does is time blocking, she is a calendar Nazi. Write down your goals. Figure out which tasks need to be completed first, put them in order by deadline and importance. Do it every day.

It's gratifying for me to read what Kim has to say. Time blocking is a huge factor in my life, along with collaboration with the group that surrounds me, drive, and the two-way street of loyalty.

I went from occupational, physical and speech therapy to starting to exercise again. Joining a gym, still using a cane for support, I knew I needed to get there as often as possible. I connected with my trainer Matt, and we hit it off from day one. I think I liked him at first because he was so big and strong (he's a power lifter). I knew that if I fell he would be able to pick me up. He was also doing very creative exercises with his people which seemed interesting to me. What I did not expect to happen was that I would get really strong. My core strength was completely non-existent, and now I'm running, lifting weights, and working out with him several days a week. It takes a village.

Matt has truly become one of my besties, not just

a trainer. His wife just delivered their twin babies, and I kept telling him to be nice to her as she was carrying two of him inside of her body! He has always given me good counsel on what I need to be doing with my life and what I don't need to be doing with my life (he has an opinion on everything, just like the majority of the people I hang with). He speaks to me like no one else can, and he gets away with it (as I mentioned earlier, he's very big and strong). Coming to terms and understanding the changes that you can physically make has been very eye opening to me, and I thank Matt for leading me down that path.

Goals can't be just for business. There has to be time for Brady, for me, for my personal life, for fun, for exploration. I block out time for that as well. Blocking time for work AND play? I never did that before. This, I'm starting to learn, is how work/life balance was supposed to be all along.

———

New Kelly decided in 2013—two and a half years after emerging from the mysterious illness and the coma—to start an independent agency. Up to that time, I had worked with a number of real estate franchise operations—RE/MAX, Coldwell Banker, and Keller Williams. I learned a lot from each of them and

I think they benefited as well from my passion, smarts, and salesmanship. As a partner in the Keller Williams franchise, I learned so much about building a team and running a business.

I watched a special on PBS once about how beavers work together and the effect they have on their families and the environment. At some point in a young beaver's life, it's customary to leave the dam, make the journey upstream, establish territory, build a home, find a mate and repeat the cycle of life. I thought that loosely described what I needed to do as a real estate professional. Leaving the nest seemed like the next step and a natural progression at the same time. Though we were associated with Keller Williams, people on the local scene identified with us as a distinct operation. We were officially called The Kelly Hager Group of Keller Williams Realty. We were getting referrals from friends, families, satisfied clients, and large corporate clients we helped with relocation services.

Before making the final decision to go independent, I had my dad come into town, and conferenced with my mom, because they knew how to make really big decisions, and I knew this was a REALLY big decision. Again, collaboration means everything.

Between my family, myself and my leadership team, we made the decision. We jumped!

Still, it was daunting. Our group, which numbered about 18 at the time, was going up against the heavy hitters. We had to build our name recognition fast. We had to invest our resources judiciously. We had to hire wisely. As you will recall, we had to do this in a real estate market still dealing with the effects of the market meltdown in 2008. As I'm reminded by the young genius Chaley Kirkpatrick, "pressure is a privilege."

We did have one clear advantage over the big boys. We could move quickly. We didn't have to go up the ladder to get anyone's permission to do anything. We could make it happen tomorrow, maybe even today. In real estate, what is of the essence? If you guessed "time," you guessed correctly.

We gathered our resources. One of them being Barbara Corcoran (from ABC's *Shark Tank*), who built her real estate business with only a $1,000 investment and later sold it for $66 million. Seemed like a great mentor to me! Off we went to New York to meet with Barbara, and learn from the best. We have met with her every year since.

Adam and Jordan, two of our more creative team members, developed our slogan: *Your Home. Your Story. Our Mission.* This business, or any business for that matter, must be client-centric. It isn't about us. It's about how we satisfy client needs through communication, trust, drive and a sense of urgency.

I hired a public relations firm to help position me as an expert in the field. Perhaps it helped that I was the hometown girl with the local brand that people could feel good about watching and supporting. That was something my parents had tapped into when they grew their independent bookstore and went up against the chains, like Borders and Barnes & Noble. People like feeling good. I envisioned being someone they could trust. Someone they could count on. I wanted to be their real estate hero!

Soon I was that real estate expert on FOX 2, NBC 5, CBS 4, and KPLR 11, who could tell you how to get your house ready for market as the buying season approached, or explain how the declining foreclosure rate was important to you as a home buyer or seller.

These were important steps, but also not uncommon in our industry. Our special sauce came from our intense and, I believe, visionary way we look at systems and work with families.

Putting all of the systems and people in place, the advertising, the promotions, the public relations, and the marketing, all comes with a large price tag. This is why we have a team making data driven decisions to increase the return on investment. We want a 4:1 return on every investment we make, from systems to the right real estate agents.

Finally, there is the people factor. Homes are an easy conversation starter. You meet a stranger at a social event. The first thing people normally ask is, "What do you do?" Once people find out what I do, they are naturally curious, even if they aren't planning to buy or sell. They might be remodeling, for instance, and wondering how much value a new powder room will add to their home.

One thing I can almost guarantee, anyone you meet at a social event is going to know someone who is buying or selling. You don't have to be very pushy to find out who those friends are. If you have a genuine conversation with someone and really show interest in "their home" and "their story," it's likely that person is going to tell their friend who is buying or selling about Kelly. "Boy, is she ever smart, trustworthy, driven, and, equally important, knowledgeable. You know what? I really liked her smile, her energy, her scarf and golly, her teeth were so white and hair was perfect too!" In all seriousness, the impact you make in these settings can be the difference between an acquaintance and a commission.

So in short, we try to be high tech, high touch and, above all, authentic and genuine.

6

Nuts and Bolts

Along the way, you've met several members of The Kelly Hager Group. At this writing, we have 40 in our bunch. We have enlisted the support of a human resources consulting firm to source and vet potential candidates. Once through that process, our leadership team conducts interviews for final selection. Building a collaborative team comes one person at a time, hand selecting the right people for the right seat.

What makes a great hire? Experience matters. Skills matter. But I look for passion, intelligence, character, loyalty, and perhaps most important, people who know how to collaborate and have a sense of urgency about implementing a vision. Hungry and determined helps as well.

Top priority... learn how to hire for your organization.

When you go through the interview process, you collect a lot of information. The first 30 days are essential to learn and communicate thoroughly. Do you remember what your new hires said their strengths were? Now you need to see if that is really where they land. Make a written plan for that employee's first 30 days with expectations and outcomes. Do this at the 60 day mark, 90 days, 180 days and after a year. The plan with each hire needs to match up with your business plan and strategy. Stay the course; focus, focus, focus. Celebrate their successes at every opportunity.

Emotional deposits....have you heard of those? Deposit in people, invest in people, work hard for your people. There are going to be times when you need to make a withdrawal. It's a constant battle that pushes and pulls. Expectations matter and to build a successful team that is immersed in the ecosystem, you must make emotional deposits, frequently. Reciprocal behavior via the two way street of loyalty and knowing that your boss is completely in your corner matters.

Speaking of focus, drive and passion, let me tell you a bit about one of the leaders on my team, Toika Collida.

We first got to know each other shortly after my return from my illness. Toika and another agent were thinking about going in another direction with their work when they sought me out for advice. I immediately took a liking to Toika because she was smart, direct and asked good questions.

Here's the way she remembers me:

Kelly was to me an enigma in a pink office—the biggest office—at Keller Williams. You looked into those windows in that office and wondered what went on in there. I knew she was leading a really productive team but I didn't really know how she operated or what she was doing behind those walls.

Then I learned that another agent was going to have a mentoring session with Kelly. She asked me if I wanted to come along.

I learned a lot at that session from Kelly, but figured we would continue to go our separate ways. Within a day or two, I got a call from her saying she was thinking of expanding her team and asked if I would like to join them. I said, "I have to think about that." In true Kelly fashion she said, "When can I call you back?"

She called me every day after that until I said yes.

Toika's family came from Norway. She was named after a Norwegian princess, and truth be told, her manner is kind of regal. She is entirely unflappable.

That isn't just a genetic inheritance, it comes from Toika's background. She was a nurse in a neonatal intensive care unit for 12 years. When you are working with babies and families in crisis every day, little else the world throws your way will seem very difficult. Toika took her crisis management skills right into real estate.

As Toika put it:

Real estate and nursing parallel each other. You take people, especially first-time homebuyers, from a place of uncertainty, stay with them, communicate honestly, and you will hopefully have a good ending. It's just as important to communicate bad news as it is to share the good news, because that's where you can lose people. They start wondering, is there something you're not telling me? You are the barometer. If they sense stress or concern in you, they are concerned. If you stay calm, they can stay calm. If you stay with them, communicate with them and they know they can count on you all the way to the end, you have done your job.

Toika has what I call drive. Everyone on my leadership team has that in common. We express it in different ways. I have vision drive. I am constantly coming up with ideas and a plan for implementation. I want them done sooner rather than later. I do not need to know every detail and I can tolerate making mistakes, as long as we are making progress. People with visionary drive enjoy taking risks and believe everything is possible.

Top Priority....Entrepreneurs' sense of urgency and first to market are differentiators.

I would be lost without people with the drive to execute the vision. These are people who leave no stone unturned, consider every detail, meet deadlines, and get everything completed with precision. Toika, Tracy, and Sharon are among many KHG team members who have those qualities.

Without vision, execution has no purpose. Without execution, the vision cannot be realized. Implementation usually takes longer or is more involved than a visionary may understand. The visionary may feel, too, that everything should happen yesterday. That's me, I always want things to happen yesterday. Whether I'm Old Kelly or New Kelly, sense of urgency is extremely important to my business.

The key to making this work is communication, participation and engagement. And it all comes back to relationships. We have talked about how KHG builds relationships with clients. Relationships with the team are equally important - *Your Career. Your Story. Our Mission.*

Making the commitment to team and driving the team to the outcome desired is essential for everyone's individual success.

Sharon runs the team's listing division, and boy does she have a lot to say. The two of us share some of the same personality traits. We work extremely hard. We are relentless in our pursuit for new business. We never make excuses for the work that we do, and we are extremely driven to succeed. She is one tough cookie, and has a heart of gold. When she's having a rough day, the best thing anyone can do is get her a nice tall pour of Chardonnay to finish up her evening.

We hounded Sharon for months before she joined the team. After she finally agreed, her start date actually hit the week after I fell out in 2010. Much like Tracy, the first few months were a little challenging. Who am I kidding? It wasn't just the first few months that were challenging! Sharon gets extreme satisfaction from building rapport with clients, negotiating great deals based on the clients' needs, and closing business.

In Sharon's words:

Coming to a team where everyone is considered family; the good, the bad, and the ugly, was extremely attractive to me. In my previous jobs, I had a high level of stress and felt very unappreciated. What I found was that when you're truly part of a team, the benefits are a shared workload, everyone is empowered, we all make decisions together, and we are not ruled with an iron fist. What I feel is that we work really hard, and manage to have fun at the same time. For example, I met Kelly in the parking lot this morning after she got off of the phone with Tracy, and we decided that Toika's birthday "networking" should begin today at 3:30 p.m. rather than 6. What we've come to understand this year is that "networking" is really just a code word for the leadership team to go out and have a big night, which ultimately truly does lead to networking with potential clients and recruiting; we like to call that productive fun.

Many would consider me an extremely tough negotiator. I've learned through my experiences with The Kelly Hager Group, we all have to fight a little bit to accomplish the desired outcomes. I have been told continuously over the years that I do need to learn to watch my tone a bit. Kelly is constantly on me for production and profitability within my division, and as I always tell her, I'm working on it! Nothing makes me happier than blowing up my numbers. In hindsight, I wish I would have made the move to KHG even sooner.

Teamwork...how do you bring out the best in everyone? How do you get everyone in sync? How do you start making gains, not just by adding, but by multiplying?

My parents had great relationships with their staff members. I learned a lot from them. My dad could be very demanding and he was often abrasive. I consider that old school, but I admire that he was never afraid to ask a lot of his staff. They stepped up because they knew he meant business and that he worked as hard, if not harder, than anyone else.

My mom was assertive in a different way. She took an interest in everyone on a personal level. She knew what I call "the big why." Why are you working here and what does it mean to you? What motivates you? What will make you happy?

I have learned that it's different for everyone. People don't work just for money, though that shouldn't be discounted as a motivator. I know what drives the leadership ladies that work for me. Tracy, Toika and Sharon all love to take girls trips to a new level, sometimes even starting as a weekend getaway, then scheduling it for a week the next time around. They love spending time with their families, traveling as much as they can. They are all just a little bit motivated by money as well, considering all three of them had daughters that left for their first year of college recently. (Yes, just in case you are curious, it has been a little emotional around this joint the last few months.)

You can enhance your relationships with your team members if you understand what they most enjoy doing, and least like doing. Personally, I love public relations work, marketing and strategizing. I get jazzed when I am in front of an audience talking about entrepreneurship. I dislike detail, back-end work. Tracy, on the other hand, loves building the office infrastructure and tracking our progress. She shuns the limelight. She is even uncomfortable when I highlight her accomplishments at a team meeting. To each his/her own, I say. Just know what it is.

Every manager has what I call a push-pull relationship with other team members. Inexperienced managers generally try to pull stuff out of their troops. I used to need minute-by-minute updates from team members on what they were up to, in part because I was curious, in part because I was wondering whether they were doing their jobs the right way.

When team members would see me coming, they wanted to change direction. Good luck with that! Our office is open and I have windows in my office so I can see what everyone is up to. I swear, if there were a blue ribbon for the real estate team most prepared for an earthquake or nuclear war, we'd have won it with all the "duck and cover" going on in our office.

As I grew as a leader, I recognized that it was counter-productive to keep my team walking on eggshells. It got in the way of their work. My team has taught me how to be a better human being, how to assert some level of balance, how to get work completed during the day so that we don't have to spend evenings on the phone dealing with the day's business.

Leadership is oftentimes on-the-job training. A huge teaching moment for me...leave it to Mike Shaw. After a really tough meeting where I was very concerned about our production, Mike shared with me the following story to put things in perspective.

There's this old joke I like to tell that has a pretty relevant lesson. It also describes how I used to approach adversity in my business versus the way I handle it now.

It's a joke about a pirate captain.

He's sailing along when the lookout in the crow's nest shouts, "Captain! Enemy ship dead ahead!"

The captain quickly locates a young deckhand. "Boy! Fetch me my red shirt!"

"Why a red shirt now, captain?" the boy asks.

"Well m'lad, should we battle the enemy and I

become wounded, I shouldn't want the rest of the men to be frightened if they see that I am bleeding."

The boy then fetches the red shirt. Later their ship emerges victorious in battle and sails on with the captured booty.

The next day, the lookout in the crow's nest shouts, "Captain! TEN enemy ships dead ahead!"

"Boy! Fetch me my brown pants!"

I think in business, you don't really need to wear the red shirt. Should you or the company become wounded, it is ok to 'bleed' a bit. And it's ok for the employees to see the blood too. That's the benefit in small failures. Seeing the one step back makes the two steps forward so much more rewarding and that's something the entire unit should share together...well, assuming you emerge victorious.

Wearing the brown pants, on the other hand, is an absolute MUST. Firstly, have the fortitude, professionalism and abdominal control to avoid both literally shitting your pants and 'freaking out' shitting your pants. A lot of the time, there's no need for it and face it, you've been in business long enough to be able to harness those behaviors and figure out a way to use all that 'freak out' energy toward a more productive resolve.

Well that was a bit graphic, but I got the point. Now we have scheduled times and processes by which we keep each other informed and accountable. Instead of my doing so much pulling, my team pushes the information to me on a scheduled basis. We are systematic.

Top priority... systematizing with critical activities will make you more profitable.

Team development means meetings and daily huddles. I have an executive leadership team meeting every Monday. I am one of the leaders of a full team meeting every Tuesday. Depending on the time of year, on Fridays our leadership group reconvenes for a brainstorming session, that includes forward-thinking, focusing on progress, and leading the pack. In between, I meet one-on-one regularly with the vice-president, director of listings, and director of buyer agent division, all smart, driven, loyal and dedicated women. It's so important to surround yourself with these types of people.

If you work in corporate America, you probably have developed your own take on staff meetings. You no doubt have been to some where your colleagues are already rolling their eyes as they gather around the conference table, or they are nodding off as the boss drones on. These meetings are frequently unfocused and counter-productive. Some are so genial that nothing important gets said, no one is accountable and nothing gets done as a result. If you're truly a corporate America lifer, you're probably already dozing off reading this paragraph. If you're still reading, congratulations! You might be the exception! Want to come work for me?

As meetings get mundane over time, it's time to break the cycle or shake it up a bit. That might mean going outside and having a meeting when it's really cold—or because it's really cold. That might mean having a big Thanksgiving feast with the office family where everyone contributes a dish. That might mean something as simple as creating a change in your daily schedule. Just don't let it get boring. When people talk about getting outside of the box, I say throw away the box. Where do you go when you're out of the box? Out of a bigger box? That never made sense to me.

Our meetings focus on goals and accomplishments that relate to executing the vision. There's a transfer of energy when our people share their successes. We ask, Where have we been? What have we learned? Where are we going? How do we get there from here?

The operations team has a daily huddle to calibrate where everyone's focus will be for the day. Much like a football huddle, it's a quick get together...minus the pads, getting in a circle and using code words for the plays we're about to run. OK, it's really nothing like a football huddle other than the fact we call it one. Since our Ops team is the central nervous system of the company, making sure the actual business is operating as it should, daily checkpoints are vital. These huddles need to be the measure to make sure no one is overloaded or taking on a task that might be better suited for another. The last thing I want to see is us running 32 option system check sweep on two, on two and watching a 65 flex wide refrigerator cleanout on one, on one. Just can't do it.

The buyer leadership team has a daily huddle as well. They break down goals for the three main key performance indicators: growth, production and profitability. Every day is different, thus some sort of update is needed. It's a sales team, so our buyer leadership team has to have their fingers on the pulse of the latest information that could make the company money. It's not micromanaging, but it is identifying where the coaching and income generation opportunities lie and being consistent with it every day. Plus it's music to my ears to hear that the sales are matching up to what they originally forecasted.

Top Priority…..Critical activities have to be completed daily.

The listing division is in constant communication with each other, as well as with the buyer division and the operations team. The buyer division feeds the listing team, and the listing team works closely with the operations team in regard to marketing and transactional support.

There is constant communication from the buyer division and the listing division to develop statistical analyses to meet all of the media opportunities we encounter.

Everyone on the operations staff is cross-trained and can fill in on a moment's notice should the need arise. The sales team couldn't function without the operations team, and the operations team would not have a lifeline without the salespeople. Everyone relies on each other.

Kathy, our Director of Operations, runs a tight ship! Her unbelievable sense of hearing ensures she doesn't miss a thing. She is a master at events, event planning, organization, agent training and one of the warmest individuals you will meet. Any time we need to "nice things up", Kathy is our girl. We're so lucky to have her.

Our other secret weapon, Buffy (who I have been great friends with since high school), does an amazing job of ensuring the contract through to the closing table is a smooth process. She is an invaluable, solution-based resource for all of our agents, both in the office and in providing showing support in a pinch. Her positive attitude and laugh is absolutely contagious.

Each member of the team has a purpose and is a direct reflection on the outcome. Everyone focusing on their strengths rather than worrying about their weaknesses will get you to the greatest level of success.

On a personal level, you can have stability and still challenge yourself by doing things a little bit differently daily. Maybe this means standing up all day in all of your meetings, maybe it means running the stairs. Maybe it means going to a quieter spot. Maybe it means running off to another country to get inspired for a few weeks... Do you have the guts to change it up or are you more comfortable plowing the same furrow?

I say follow your dreams. If you don't know what your dreams are, then it's helpful to work for other people and start defining what you want by narrowing down the pieces of the jobs that you like the best, building on your strengths and understanding your weaknesses. Then jump out of your box and throw it away.

7

Go Big or Go Home!

You've heard these cliches.

No pain. No gain.

No guts. No glory.

At The Kelly Hager Group, I'm fond of saying, Go big, or go home.

In short, it takes guts to be an entrepreneur. If you don't want to go big, going home may mean returning to the cocoon of corporate America. In corporate America, you can have a good week or a bad week, a good month or a bad month, but always know that at the end of the week or the end of the month, a paycheck will be waiting for you. In corporate America, you can get a big idea, but by the time you get the many permissions it will take to run with it, you may have lost time and traction. Only so many big ideas will actually get done, and far more will never see the light of day.

Many people are a great fit in corporate America. It's safe. If you are looking for structure, security and establishment, then you ought to jump right in. It's not a bad place to start. As you work your way up the ladder, you will learn a lot about how to run your own business someday if you have an entrepreneurial mindset.

That's what happened to me.

Without really realizing it, I began to think like a business owner while still working for a corporate entity. The first thing I did was understand the expectations my managers had for me. I made it my goal to exceed those expectations, blow them out of the water! I got so good at going above and beyond that one of my employers put a cap on my commissions. Twice, but who's counting? Obviously I was. Shame on them the first time, shame on me the second. That ticked me off. But it helped push me more toward thinking about owning my own business, where no glass ceiling existed, where my only limitations were in how far I could stretch my own mind.

In corporate America, I came to be considered one

of the most aggressive sales people in the room. My numbers were good and my track record was strong. Soon my bosses were inviting me to take the stage to address hundreds of my colleagues. If your boss and your boss's boss believe in you, you can climb any mountain. That is so rewarding. Not only do you want to succeed for yourself, but you also want to succeed for the team.

This gave me the belief that I could start my own company. But as an entrepreneur and owner, you find that it can be counterproductive to be the smartest person in the room, or at least to act that way. You can't know everything unless you're that guy who won something like 743 *Jeopardy* shows in a row, so you need people to fill in your knowledge gaps. I quickly realized I'd crash and burn without my peers' business acumen.

Development of your action plan should include key performance indicators. Think about your business for a second. Do you have three to five key strategies, and the objectives to get you to the outcome/results for which you are looking?

Let me provide you with a couple of examples:

It had been 15 months since the onset of my extended hospital hibernation. There was no question what needed to be done. Fundamentally, I had two choices.

#1 - I could go big. What was big? What is "blowing it up?" How in the hell am I going to do this? Anyway, that was the option. To go big. I decided I would figure it out later.

#2 - I could go home. During this decision making process, I realized I was already at home, so this made option #1 a much more appealing solution.

We weren't making enough money. We had to make a decision about whether to commit 10 percent of our revenues to a lead generation system. The system had to work or we were going to have to dissolve the company.

As a facet of going big, the visionary, me, wanted to spend three times the amount that we actually spent on the lead generation system. I could see the potential. I knew it would take a while to realize that potential, but the quicker we got going, the sooner we would get there.

Fortunately, the room I was in had some very intelligent people there as well. They were the execution drivers, the folks who have to think about the details and be realistic about how long it takes to get things done. I learned we did not have enough staff to be able to execute at a high enough level. We met in the middle on the number of leads and moved forward. I felt like our business was the mutant offspring of the tortoise and the hare, but ultimately it turned out to be a pace fast enough to extract the maximum amount of benefit.

Every entrepreneur goes through a period of wondering, "Is this the right path?" When there is too little cash flow, the calls you make can be excruciating. So you have to ask yourself, quite simply, "Do I have the guts to be an entrepreneur?"

As Colin Powell says, "Great leaders are almost always great simplifiers, who can cut through argument, debate, and doubt to offer a solution everybody can understand."

We are a results-driven group that knows what we have to do to get the job done. Implementation is expected.

Here's another example:

It's now two and a half years past the onset of my illness. We had to decide whether to break from our existing broker and set up our own shop, Kelly Hager Group Real Estate Services, or stay put. Our execution drivers knew the back-end systems and to set up our independent shop, it was going to take more time and effort than I was imagining. No one tried to talk me out of taking the leap, but together we put together a step-by-step approach that enabled us to go big instead of going home.

––––––

I've talked about going big, taking a calculated risk and executing. These are fundamentals for any entrepreneur. But then there is growth. Successful companies never rest on their laurels. They went big and now the challenge is to stay big. They innovate relentlessly. They don't just hire more staff, they train them and help them grow as professionals and as people. People follow leaders because they want to. They have been inspired and believe in the ideal.

Importantly, they stay focused, but do not get narrow-minded.

If you are baseball fan, you know that many good pitchers feature a fastball, but if that's all they threw, batters would catch up to that pitch no matter how hard pitchers hurled the ball. The great ones have a repertoire of as many as four pitches, often a fastball, a change-up, a slider, a curveball.

Likewise, The Kelly Hager Group has maintained at least four streams of revenue. To keep up the baseball metaphor, each requires a different grip or approach.

Our current revenue streams are:

- Lead generation systems

- Spheres of Influence

- Public Relations

- Events

- Break down the streams of revenue where profitability is the most attainable. Where are the barriers? How do you work around them? Having the right people in place means everything.

We have already talked a bit in previous chapters about our lead generation system and how we use spheres of influence. You will recall that our lead generation system is a means of bringing in potential homebuyers and sellers who are already online or using social media to research opportunities. That's not only high tech, but vital tech. It's the paradigm shift in real estate in today's world.

Our spheres of influence are high touch—the people we know and meet in our everyday lives.

We use events and public relations to bring in even more people. These widen our spheres of influence and establish our brand, and also bring people into our lead generation systems so that we can maintain contact with these clients over time.

No matter what business you're in, this applies. Lead generation systems are simply pay-per-click and search engine optimization on websites. Leveraging this kind of technology in today's distracted and digitally addicted world is not to be ignored. Why? Because if it's not us, it will be someone else capturing the market share. That's not how you go bigger.

At the events, we have the opportunity to speak to people about their home buying and selling needs. Outgoing and engaging personalities are paramount when you're in the public eye. Salespeople will tell you they're much more effective face-to-face, so this is a great venue to not only go bigger, but to put our best people in the environment that best suits their strengths.

An example: We do wedding shows in January and July. This puts me and our team in front of 1,500 to 2,000 people at a 10-hour event. In keeping with the bridal theme, we call ourselves The Real Estate Match Makers. It's not just gathering data from these people, it's taking that data and using it to our advantage.

Top Priority... add contacts to your database every single day. If you're not adding, you're subtracting.

We also sponsor amphitheater movie nights in our community, where anywhere from 3,000 to 7,000 people attend and get a taste of The Kelly Hager Group.

In a sense, we are creating a funnel. While not everyone at our events is in the market for a home, we can expect at least 30-40 will fall through that funnel and become potential clients.

The wedding shows are an asset for us in another way. January is a time when cash flow is light and we are less busy. The shows give us something to do that generates business and improves profitability while other firms might be idling. We get ready for the show between Christmas and New Year's Day. No down time at The Kelly Hager Group.

Once we have made contact with our 2,000 potential customers, we drop the most interested into our lead generation system. We get them on a drip campaign, followed up by personal contact. We convert those contacts into listings and contracts.

Events can be extremely profitable for any sales organization. We always look for a 4:1 return on our investments. Selecting the correct events is what's important. Remember who you are trying to reach—the key demographic—and go after it. In circumstances like this, let the data help you make those decisions.

With enthusiasm and energy the possibilities are endless. Bring it. When you are at an event, out with a client, talking on the phone with a new potential client, your energy and enthusiasm determine your level of success.

———

That brings us to public relations.

We are quite well known, perhaps better known than a lot of other real estate firms that have been around a whole lot longer.

Like most companies, we have purchased time on television, but public relations, at least in part, is the art of drawing attention to yourself through free media.

To do that we have positioned ourselves as a resource. We are considered experts in our field and invited to speak on television, radio, newspapers, magazines, and online because we are knowledgeable, not because we can sell (though we are very good at that too). Share your time and expertise. Most people really need the help.

We began developing speaking engagements in 2014 with corporations, university students and associations fostering entrepreneurship. In 2015, I am booked not only nationally but internationally as well. Speaking with other entrepreneurs is so rewarding for me. Just as my mentors have helped accelerate my business, I am looking to do the same for others. Everyone has opportunity. Take advantage of your resources. Efficiency and profitability can excel if you surround yourself with the right people and if you work with consultants and mentors who have done what you want to do.

As Lou Holtz says, "Your talent determines what you can do. Your motivation determines how much you are willing to do. Your attitude determines how well you do it." I love this guy. When I was in college, I had the opportunity to attend several Notre Dame football games, and there is nothing more thrilling than to see 60,000 people cheering for one man. Shocking to see all of those people screaming and raving at this coach that was able to obtain exceptional results. How do you do that in your business?

In public relations, it's important to hit the market with everything you've got. And in today's lightspeed world, perception is reality.

———

There are rules for growth in any organization.
My rules for growth:

1. Invest in the right people and the right systems, business and personal. This might include money. This might include development time. This might include your heart.

2. Choose people for who they are, how they can contribute to the team, and how the team can contribute to them.

3. Grow business as quickly as you can with people that are solution-based and the right fit, and systems that fit a profitable model with a 4:1 return.

4. Do not hire just warm bodies.

5. Increase personal growth by reading every day.

6. Connect with someone smarter than you every day.

7. Step out of your comfort zone every day.

8. Learn something about yourself every day.

9. Reflect every day.

What are your rules for growth? What does that look like for you and your life? Personal growth? Business growth? Do you know when enough is enough?

You have to have systems in place in order to be efficient and profitable. The equal part to that is working with families; understanding their needs, being compassionate and caring, having excellent negotiation skills, and helping them move to the next chapter in their lives. Listening, always listening.

Top priority... If you're the smartest person in the room, you're in the wrong room!

8

Team Guts

Earlier, I talked to you about guts and entrepreneurship. What it takes to win in a highly competitive world.

I was addressing you as an individual and sharing my particular story with you. But unless you are a one-man or a one-woman band, it's going to take a team for you to succeed.

You will need what I call Team Guts.

You will have to find the right people to join your team and once you do, you will all have to get comfortable with each other—but not too comfortable. You will all have to want to take risks and sky dive together.

The people on my team made the difference when I was really sick and incapacitated. The difference was between going bankrupt or building our business into a powerhouse. I like these people. I love these people. I rely on these people. I would go to the end of the earth for these people; that's what a true team does for each other. The older I get, the more I understand that relationships are essential, not only in your private life but also in your business life. Nothing is more exciting than to see people succeed both professionally and personally.

Top Priority...understand who you are, and understand who you need. There are a variety of personality assessments available for you to use in this process.

We have a sisterhood. We are forward thinkers. We never let the past dictate the future. We never gossip because we don't have time and it's bad for the ecosystem. We're never afraid to do the stuff that matters, and we make time for it. We actively try new things. We like to learn. We like to teach. We love thinking time. We love to question. We love to explore. We love to experiment (a little bit anyway). We love to cross-pollinate ideas, and we are truly there for each other in any and every circumstance. By building a team like this, life is so much easier. Whether we are in a brainstorming meeting, out "networking," or having tough conversations, we all know that we're on this journey together. Who could ask for anything more than that?

In your organization, how do you develop camaraderie like this? Development takes time, effort, participation by everyone, and a willingness to achieve the outcomes desired. Everyone needs to buy-in to the vision and what it takes to get there. Then and only then, share, discuss and develop ideas together to achieve the desired results.

Growth, development, production and retention are our top priorities. The leadership team understands that these four "buckets" are everything to our organization. Anyone who runs a successful business would agree. If those are the top four, and everything underneath falls into a bucket, then let's talk about strategy development for each bucket.

Growth: For our organization, adding agents on a monthly basis is very important. It's great to add agents, but attracting the right people is the most important. You've got to make sure your people can not only do the job, but perform it well. Quick, would you rather have a new Ferrari or 11 Yugos? Exactly.

Development is equally important. Imagine walking

into a job on the first day and the boss slapping you on the back as you walk out onto the sales floor saying, "I'll see you in a few weeks. Go get 'em, Tiger!" Has that model ever turned anyone into a rock star producer?

Investing time and energy in your people up front is a differentiator, not addressing the development down the line. Confidence corresponds with successful production. Success breeds confidence. Our development at KHG includes training, coaching, mentoring and supporting agents as they walk through the process. We love everyone on the team, and that means everyone gets what they need.

Production: Helping team members get into significant production is imperative. With our model, we hire full-time agents. We want people who want real estate as a career. These agents can produce 2+ transactions consistently on a monthly basis with the systems we have in place. After the significant time/financial investment, and our dedication to their success, they stay!

Retention comes from a lot of caring support and providing opportunities for people to succeed at the highest level. Most people tend to stick around when they do a good job, make money and realize they work for an exceptional organization.

Business gurus often speak about differentiating your product from the others so that it stands out, so that it sells. Remember Steve Jobs? Didn't he have a few great ideas to make him stand out? You should Google him.

To quote Richard Branson, founder of the Virgin Group and another fairly smart billionaire, "Innovation does not come from taking a path already charted. It comes from thinking differently and challenging the status quo. Look at history's most successful brands, the ones that stand out are those that did not just add to the game, but disrupt it and change it for good. Apple, Google, Facebook and Tesla—each of these names have reimagined products and services to create cult followings. The key to their success in achieving such followings is that they have not just sold a product or service, but an idea. Virgin is more than just a group of products and services—it is an attitude, a lifestyle, a strong identity."

Teamwork and guts are what differentiates The Kelly Hager Group. Our tagline speaks to our clients: *Your Home. Your Story. Our Mission.* Our purpose is to serve our clients. My clients are my leadership team and my agents: *Your Career. Your Story. Our Mission.* My job is to bring in opportunity for them. Their clients are all of the wonderful buyers and sellers who they work with.

Let me give you a couple of examples:

Real estate firms grow and prosper in large measure by attracting top agents. The more agents you have the greater the number of listings, and ultimately the commissions that put bread on the table for everyone. To attract agents, we needed to stand out. What would make us different?

Well, one thing we noticed is that we offer a very different experience for our agents, which means they can offer a very different experience for their clients. The business opportunities and support they receive is unique to us.

We spend a lot of time and resources on our agents and on our listings. We train our agents relentlessly, and we offer them marketing opportunities they can't find elsewhere. Mastery of dialogues, market conditions, negotiations and principles on how to expand their own business and development are constant reminders how preparation leads to the separation. It's not hard being better than the rest. What is hard is making the commitment to be better every single day.

For instance, we spend a great deal of money participating in bridal shows and other community events, which gets our agents in front of thousands of people. Other brokerage houses may encourage their agents to attend these events, but attendance and participation comes at the agents' expense. Our public relations efforts, getting our name out there in big and impressive ways, accrues to the benefit of each agent. Agents considering whether to jump on board with my firm or another have to appreciate who is creating the most buzz and the most opportunities in the marketplace. It takes guts, often in the form of putting money and resources at risk, to do that.

But team guts works both ways. When it's your turn to shoot the ball, everyone on the team needs you to score. If you don't have what it takes, it's immediately noticeable.

Our agents have the following set of core competencies in common:

- Flexibility/adaptability

- Consistency

- Collaboration

- Honesty

- Confidence

- Drive/ambition

- Persuasive communication skills

- Relationship building skills

As you're thinking about your company, what are the core competencies that make the most sense? What are your greatest strengths and where do you need to make up the difference? How can you make the greatest impact on your company in the most efficient way possible? It all comes back to surrounding yourself with the right team of people.

How do we know if an agent has what it takes? We take a close look at the agents we consider by doing a two-hour interview and vetting them through an HR consultant. It's impossible to know just how good an agent will be until they begin to work with us. We prescreen 10-13 candidates for every role we fill.

You will notice that "experience" is not on the list of core competencies. What is experience in real estate? Tenure? Production? Specialization? It's very subjective really, and I think if you force yourself to define experience, it sort of limits who your future players will be. To be sure, experience in the real estate business can be an asset. Other experiences can be just as beneficial. When I worked at the pharmaceutical company, I didn't have any pharmaceutical experience, and they viewed that as a benefit as they wouldn't have to undo what another company had taught me. I operate the same way. Agents who have been in the business for a long time are so accustomed to doing things their way, that it's hard for them to bridge the gap to the way our ecosystem works. We are forward thinking and progressive, with a tremendous sense of urgency. "Traditional" agents can be quite the opposite.

We find that former teachers do very well because they are at once nurturers and communicators. They are also highly organized and process oriented. Don't forget, they've had the tough job of negotiating with kids on a daily basis, and in most cases have won! We have a very process-based system, and teachers fit that mold well.

Another new agent is quickly becoming one of our best. She comes from the health care industry. We met her at a job fair and it took several months to reel her in.

She had to put together a flow chart and a spreadsheet that would help her analyze whether she would make enough money to take the leap. We liked that about her. The work ethic, drive and sense of urgency she possesses surfaced the moment she walked through the door.

Let me give you an example of how she operates. On day one, I will send her a lead.

She texts me back: "I'm calling her right now."

In a few minutes, I get another text. "No answer. I'm sending her a text."

A bit later, I hear back again. "She got back to me, she's pre-approved and I'm showing her a home this afternoon."

And so it goes, high communication. I get regular updates from her on this valuable lead until she has landed the buyer. You can imagine that if she is keeping me apprised, she must be doing twice as much to keep the client on board. So here she is not just demonstrating consistency, one of the core competencies, but also is building a relationship. This will pay off with the client, who will come to trust her and know that she is on top of things and has her back. This will pay off with me, because I am going to be so inclined to share my next lead with her because I have the confidence that she will follow through.

We have another agent who had once been a client, and relocated to our area from Kansas City. We knew right away that she was going to be a rock star. She is so thorough and organized, full of compassion, drive, and a sense of urgency. Her caring and compassionate nature builds clients for life. It's so rewarding to watch how much success people can have and make such a great impact for their families financially.

We've all had clients for whom we need to go above and beyond the call of duty on their behalf. The agent I was just talking about had a client who was a single mom, and was so excited to close on the sale of her first home. Unfortunately, on the day before closing it was pouring down rain when they had to do their final walk-through. The mud they had to wade through was so deep that they actually lost their shoes in it.

Going above and beyond should be standard practice in any solid organization. Sometimes it's just the little things, but sometimes you have to go to the end of the earth, and in either case it's what makes the difference.

———

Flexibility is another one of our core competencies. In our firm, we constantly try new things. Not all of them work. One of my mentors, Matt, helped me accept failure. He introduced me to the concept of failing forward—learning from the experience and moving ahead. He recommended what he calls 52 course corrects a year.

This is another concept that separates The Kelly Hager Group from the pack. Many companies review goals and accomplishments on a quarterly or annual basis. At best this can be a recipe for slow, steady progress. At worst, atrophy and bankruptcy. If you want your organization to build momentum and grow rapidly, it's important to ask where you stand every week. Then you can course correct and get there more quickly.

Initially, one of our biggest mistakes was in not hiring the right people. Once we course corrected and understood what the necessary core competencies truly were, problem solved!

Developing the streams of revenue based on statistical analysis versus what "felt right", was a huge course correct. For us, people transitioning from one chapter in their lives to another are the people we need to focus on. Typically, those are the people that will be moving and really need our help.

Understanding where your company needs to focus resources is essential to growing profitability.

Top Priority.... 52 course corrects a year.

———

Perhaps I should say 52 course corrects in a day, or even an hour. I am going to share with you some stories from my staff that are humorous and even hilarious, but also demonstrate the resilience we honor at KHG. They will also shine a light—sometimes not all that flattering—on the real estate business. You had better be one tough hombre if you want to get in this line of work, because it's the Wild West out there.

This first story from our agent, Elizabeth, comes under the category of "never let them see you sweat."

I was showing high-rise condos downtown, Elizabeth

recounts. That is hard enough. But to get the key for the first unit that I wanted to show, I had to get into another unit in the same building which was also being shown.

I was given a code to get into the front door of the building, which did not work. Fortunately some residents let us in.

Then we take the elevator and go to the 16th floor and go to the stairwell where there's a Supra for unit 1604. (The Supra is a lock box that real estate agents use to secure the key to a property that another real estate agent is showing.) I open 1604 and follow my instructions. The key to the unit I wanted to show is in a bowl under the kitchen sink. Finally we get to that unit and my clients take a look around. Afterward, I have to repeat the process to put all of the keys back.

Not done yet, however. My clients want to look at another condo unit a block away.

This is where it got crazy. Once again the code to get into the building didn't work. Again a resident let us in. Now we have to look for the Supra. My instructions said the supra was inside the second set of double doors. There was nothing. So I thought maybe it is on the door to the unit. We went to the elevator. There is a set of double doors with a code lock to get to the elevator. No code was given to me. While we were standing there a resident came out and let us in the double doors and *we got into the elevator.*

So far so good. We went to the appropriate floor. Alas, no Supra. I told my clients to have a seat in a vestibule in the hallway while I called the listing agent to see where the Supra was.

Of course she didn't answer. So I went back down the elevator to look around. As the elevator opened on the main floor, I remembered that I didn't have the code to get the double doors open again to get back in the elevator. Luckily, I found some phone books that had just been delivered to the building. I put the phone books in the double door to hold it open.

Now I am in the lobby looking for the Supra. There it is! It's hanging outside on a rail. I would have to go through another two sets of double doors to get it. And I didn't have the code to get back in. Hey, no problem. I put my purse in the first set of doors to hold it open. Only one more set of double doors to conquer. I put my leg in the door and reached my entire body out to get the Supra. Mission accomplished!

I went back in, collected my purse, put the phone books back and took the elevator to the floor where my clients were waiting. Very calmly I said, "found it."

They had no idea what I just went through to get that key.

As it turned out, the clients purchased neither one of those condos. I'm happy to say we have formed a strong bond. They have to sell their home before they can buy. Oddly, they had listed their home with another firm. Now they have switched to KHG. Going above and beyond for your client, no matter the outcome, really makes a difference.

The next story comes from Cindy, another one of our buyer agents. She has been with me for five years. It is unusual in that circumstances developed so quickly. It is typical in that we frequently must act as a buffer between clients who for one reason or another are at odds.

Not long ago I was out showing homes to George and Monica (not their real names.) The couple was following me from house to house in their car while I drove ahead in mine. At one stop, George got out of the car and said, "Will you take me home. I have had it with Monica and we are breaking up."

Now George has a great sense of humor, so I thought he was teasing me.

I said, "For real?"

He said, "Yes, I just can't stand her anymore."

I said, "For real, for real?"

He said, "If you don't want to, I will call a cab."

I kept looking back at the car trying to get Monica to look at me but she just kept looking down. Needless to say I took George home. Awkward. After we got to his apartment, we talked a bit, then he said he wanted to go back to the house we had just come from, back to Monica. Halfway there, he called me on his cell from his car to say he was getting back together with Monica. Guess you got to break up to make up.

Sue, one of our relocation specialists, is, of course, most often relocating humans. But there are others to consider as well.

I was contacted by a relocation firm to help one of their clients moving to St. Louis from Texas. They warned me it was not going to be an easy task. I contacted the client and he told me he had two potbelly pigs that would be relocating with his family. The pigs each weighed 100 lbs. and were 14 and 15 years old. Their names were Precious and Princess.

I had less than a week to find the client some homes to see so I could time it with his visit to St. Louis. I started contacting municipalities to see if pigs were allowed. Amazing that St. Charles, St. Peters, and Dardenne

Prairie allowed pigs as long as they were pets and not used as livestock. Wildwood also allowed them but you had to be on five acres or more. We looked at 10 homes in two days and picked out his future home. My client will be closing soon and his family and pigs will be joining him the first of the year. Needless, to say we are all looking forward to meeting Precious and Princess. I expect those piggies will be providing referrals.

Mike, our lead buyer specialist, broke into the business the hard way.

These two stories came from the same trip out with the same client. As I think about it, this was my first ever client and maybe even the first few homes I ever showed...

House 1: *Unlock door. As I'm opening it to let the client in, I see an entirely empty and dimly lit great room with only an elderly man in a lazy boy rocking semi slowly to what? Am I in a Metallica video and are you creeped out yet? The old man is not even looking at us. This elevates the creep factor by about 5. He just waves his arm over his head and all scruffy sounding, yells "COME ON!" I look down and there's a dog. Sweet. I like dogs. The dog and I IMMEDIATELY make eye contact. I would imagine by this dog's body language that I presented a SEVERE threat because it showed all of its teeth and* began snarling as dogs do when they are about ready to bite your hands, feet or possibly genitalia. I changed my mind. I don't like dogs now.

I hesitate and ask, 'This one friendly?"

"HE'S FINE!", the old man thunders.

"Sir, he appears to be pretty upset. His teeth are showing."

This is when it gets astoundingly awkward. The old man then turns to us and screams louder than he was yelling before, "GINNNNNGERRRR!" (Ginger? Really? I would have guessed Annihilator or Psycho.)

Fight or likely flight was my main concern, but since this was my first trip out with this client, I didn't want to look like a huge wimp, so I suggested to my buyer that we take a QUICK lap through the house.

We walk around the house in complete silence and decided we'd seen enough after maybe 90 seconds. Feedback for the listing agent was, "Great curb appeal. Priced well. Could have shown better without the scary old man and possibly rabid dog. Best of luck!"

House 2: We enter a very nice atrium ranch. Granite flooring in great shape, three-car garage and spacious bedrooms. We head downstairs to examine the rec room, kitchenette and advertised "sleeping area." The sleeping area, oddly enough did not have the lights turned on unlike the rest of the home. I casually flip on the light as my buyer is walking down the stairs.

Lo and behold I do not have the pleasure of viewing a staged bedroom. Instead I am greeted with an incredibly large man lying face down in the bed. No covers. No clothes except for the tidy whities. (Yeah I looked long enough to notice. Don't judge.)

I half expected to turn around and bump chests with the CSI: St. Louis cast members, but quickly realized that it would just be better to run. I meet my buyer mid-steps and in a mixture of yelling and whispering at the same time say, "Just GO!!!!"

I debrief the buyer. We concluded that flipping on the light should have awakened the man. But he hadn't stirred. It was dawning on me that I might need to alert the authorities on a possible situation in the "sleeping area."

I called the listing agent at level 9 freak out mode. Told her there might be a dead guy in the house. She must have handled it I guess, because I never heard back from her again.

I did not leave feedback for this home. Guess what? My client did not make an offer.

Top priority ... As an agent, you are helping people with the largest purchase of their lives. Engagement, participation, sense of urgency and communication are everything.

9

The Chic-ocracy

Kim remembers a jaw-dropping moment with me.

A gentleman had come into my office and was pitching me on a proposal.

We had just moved into our new offices, and Kim, as my assistant, had a desk on the other side of my office. She couldn't help overhearing the conversation, which was short. Kim considered it brutally short.

"He was so nice and friendly," Kim said. "And Kelly, after listening to him for maybe just a minute, simply said, 'Nope, we're not interested. You can stop talking.'

"I thought, oh my gosh, that is so harsh. Why couldn't she have done a little la-de-da to make it more polite?"

Kim never said a word to me about that encounter. She reflected on it over time as she gathered momentum in her own career, as a woman in business.

"At the time, I was a lot softer," Kim recalled. "I began to recognize that you can't always please people. If you are constantly teeter-tottering with them, you are going to lose focus. Sometimes you have to bring out that tough side so you can move on, not waste your time or their time."

That's true for everyone, but maybe especially women, Kim believes.

"This is Kelly Hager's office," she said. "Her name is on the door. This is her space and in this space she can't let anyone walk on her or compromise her vision. Kelly has the biggest heart ever. If she has bad news, she will not sugarcoat it for you.

"You can't sugarcoat things, especially as a woman."

I couldn't agree more.

Toughness, which is often associated with men, is an important quality when it comes to women succeeding in business. It's not the only quality. Many of the attributes that are commonly associated with women work just as well. Even better. Those should not be left out of the equation.

Among those attributes:

Time management. Women can walk, chew gum, rub their tummies, pat their heads, take care of the kids and take care of business. We focus on the task at hand, get it done, and then move on to the next.

Collaboration. Men are known to be competitive, which sometimes means caring too much about who gets the credit. Women more easily focus on getting everything completed. We have the huddles every morning to ensure everyone is on the same page and not overwhelmed. There is so much to accomplish that there is no time to get overloaded. We stay in the top 20% of the critical activities 60-70% of the time. The morning huddles really allow us to do this.

Delegation. This builds on collaboration. Everyone carries the ball. Everyone Is responsible for their piece and the outcome. People who delegate effectively cannot only get more tasks completed, they are showing trust in their colleagues. This is repaid in so many ways. People work harder, they are more loyal. They are far more invested in the outcome. They think like owners.

Passion. We love what we do and aren't afraid to express it. Men can be just as passionate, but can also be more reserved. At KHG, we get excited about our accomplishments. We celebrate them. We party. We talk enthusiastically about taking the next big step. We use !!!!! in our communications everyday!!!

So it shouldn't come as a shock to you that all four of the people on our KHG executive leadership team are women. Along with me they are Tracy, Toika, and Sharon, all of whom you have met previously in this book.

Now I'd like to introduce you to Mike.

A guy.

Mike is one of our lead buyer specialists. He reports to Toika and oversees a portion of the training and development for our staff and agents. Aside from our agents, he is just one of four men currently on the team.

Mike has an exceptional background. He worked in the mortgage industry for the better part of a decade and he has also been a certified teacher for several years. So he understands the real estate market and can teach many facets of the sales process to our agents.

In the mortgage industry, Mike reported mostly to men. So you may wonder if there was a moment of transition when he entered his first female dominated leadership meeting. Like a wolf earning his place among a foreign pack of alpha-females, Mike accepted his seat at the table. One man doesn't change it all. It was still a chic-ocracy.

He laughs at that notion, but then talks about where he came from and how he fit into KHG, gender and all.

I came to The Kelly Hager Group in July 2012, after having been an independent agent for several years. At that point, I really was trying to reinvent myself. I had worked in the mortgage industry until 2006 when the economy began to go sideways. The mortgage business didn't exploit all of my strengths and I wasn't too passionate about the job, so it seemed logical to pursue a more fulfilling career.

It was then I decided to get my real estate license. I knew building my business would take time, so to make ends meet, I pursued another passion in teaching. I worked also as a substitute teacher, teaching a high school business course. Along the way, I went back to school and got a master's degree in teaching. Understanding that two full-time careers were at stake, and having a lot of passion for both industries, my goal was to juggle both until one took over as the more lucrative endeavor. Lucrative and teaching aren't two words that normally go together, so suffice it to say, real estate emerged victorious.

I had the buyer side of a transaction that happened to be a KHG listing and Sharon was the listing agent. We had such a smooth process together, that Sharon suggested I meet her and Kelly to discuss joining the team. By then I knew of Kelly's reputation. I had worked at Keller Williams and had seen her office. She had the most bedazzle I had ever seen in a real estate office, so many colors, mostly pink, shiny stuff and balloons and a whole team packed into a pretty small space. I'm wondering, "What is the secret here?" She seemed to have so much going on. All of this seemed to be the void in my own real estate business. I had to know how she got to that level.

As I learned more, I saw that Kelly had undergone a reinvention herself since her illness. We were both trying to do more. We had hit a wall in our careers and even life itself, where we had to start over. So after Sharon made the introductions, we talked for two hours. Kelly talked about her vision and how she wanted her growth plan to go. We would have our own office building one day and we were just going to blow it up. I talked about my own goals and what strengths I could bring to the team.

I joined as an agent and within a year, I was brought on as the lead buyer specialist. What struck me about working for so many women? High velocity. Lots of things going on all at once. I was more process-oriented. I came from a world of procedures in the mortgage industry and even more procedures from the education world. I love data and statistics, and in real estate, it's more than enough to be dangerous in terms of educating your client. In meetings and company development, it's the same way only a little more cautious because it seems like so much more is at stake. If it's up to me, we take data-driven looks before leaping.

The other thing I noticed is that women like to talk things out. Men never like to ask for directions, let alone talk about the reasons why we're lost in the first place. We know where we're going. Trust us. Women want to have a discussion. We have a lot of brainstorming sessions, which I like. What I really enjoy is the execution. I want to build it. I also like putting together the instruction manual so others can join in the execution.

I have learned a lot working with women. You want to make sure when you speak that you are saying something in a way that you intended it to be heard. They are sensitive. I should have learned all of this from my wife, but I think I had to learn the hard way on the job a few times! That said, along with the gender gap, I've learned a lot is interpreted a much different way than I

had intended. I am pretty sensitive myself, so I do care
what others think. In our leadership meetings, I have to
be careful not to assert any dominance even if I do think
I have the right answer."

Then Mike chuckled, "Because I gotta watch out. I'm
outnumbered."

Well that's certainly true within our office. Toika says,
"At the end of the day it's a man's world."

She adds, "It's nice to break those boundaries. Some
of our most successful agents are women. When it
comes to tough negotiations, they can go in for the kill
in the nicest way possible."

That said, we don't go into negotiations with a
"winner take all" mindset, it gets you nowhere to use this
technique.

"I am a solid, aggressive negotiator; I am not a bully,"
Toika said. "I take a different approach. Let's make it
reasonably fair for all parties." As long as we get more
than 60-70% of the win, we are happy.

Women face expectations that men do not. God
bless the men who are nurturers and are very present
in their children's lives. God bless the men who cook
and put dinner on the table. Amen, we need more of
those. God bless the men who do the laundry and make
sure the house is tidy. In our world these men get extra
credit. As for women, this is simply what comes with their

territory. Many women who fall short in a given day in these areas are prone to feel guilty.

Old Kelly failed to recognize that her women staffers carried the extra weight of these family expectations. Old Kelly didn't account for what people call the work/life balance.

New Kelly recognizes that it's important to most women and many men to be at home with their family for dinner. Weekends are sacred for most, sometimes in a religious or spiritual way, but frequently as a means to creating memories and experiences that keep family bonds strong.

That's why it is so important for everyone on our team to focus on time management. We talk quite a bit about how to block out our day so that we are focused on what needs to get accomplished and how those duties affect our profitability. That frees up the time to be at home or at an athletic field or driving a car pool when it's necessary. More importantly, if we have ticked every box on our checklist while at work, it frees up our minds to actually be present in the moment when we are with our families. Only then can we really hear what our spouses and children are saying and, in that psychic way that wives and mothers have, only then can we become attuned to their needs.

I would not be a woman in business without role

models. They don't all have to be women. My dad was a great role model, especially as a visionary. He taught me how to turn dreams into reality. When you are a female, nothing gives you a greater sense of possibility than finding another woman who has been there and done that. My mom was that first role model. Coming of age in the early 1960s, when so few women went to business school or owned their own business, she displayed guts and courage that I could hardly appreciate as a child. Today there's hardly a day that passes or a decision that I make when I don't reflect on how she would handle a situation. If I am still wondering, all I have to do is pick up the phone and she is there for me.

I hope you are blessed with a great mom, like mine. I hope as well that you find a mentor who is not your mom. For me that's Barbara Corcoran, who is not in any way like a mom (except to her own kids). Moms have a way of taking your emotional temperature then calibrating what they say accordingly. Barbara doesn't take your temperature. She just tells you frankly what she thinks. She is candid, someone who wants to see you succeed and will share truths that will help you get there.

Barbara has the street cred to do that. She was a diner waitress when she borrowed $1,000 from a boyfriend and got into the real estate business in the toughest market in the world, New York. She built her company into a $6-billion business. Now you can see her on *Shark Tank*, the show in which fledgling entrepreneurs pitch their ideas to successful business people who decide whether to help them out with financial backing.

Barbara first came to my attention when I would watch the *Today* show as I was getting going in the morning. Tracy would be there with me at my home office and we would marvel both at her expertise and the down-to-earth way in which she expressed herself.

For example, in an interview with Matt Lauer in 2010 during a down market, Barbara came on with five great tips for selling your house. Number 5 focused on the three key spaces: the kitchen, the living room and the front façade, which is one area people frequently overlook.

Soon, I was dreaming ... How can we get Barbara to work with us? For a fee, a very large fee, she would come for a visit. We didn't have the dough to afford that, but what if we were to visit her? I sent her an e-mail proposing just that. There are many ways to get what you want.

To my surprise, she got right back to us and agreed. Eight weeks later we were sitting in her office.

Tracy and I flew up to New York for that first encounter. We were promised an hour, but she spent a few hours, and we were blown away. She was fast paced, smart, and taking no prisoners!

Barbara asked us about every member of our team. And she didn't mince words.

After my description of one team member, Barbara simply said: "Fire her."

"What? What are you basing that on?"

"The whole tone of your voice changed when you were talking about her. I can tell you she's no good for your organization."

We did dismiss that team member. More importantly, Tracy and I learned from Barbara how to bring more focus to our thinking, to hone in on profitability and to feel more confident about the tasks we undertook.

Since then we have met with Barbara every year, and I have included additional team members as well.

Mentoring with Barbara Corcoran was instrumental in my business taking off; it's so important to meet with those who have done what you want to do. This is a differentiator.

Top Priority....Meet with people who have already done what you want to do.

One of my favorite ways to spend my time is mentoring others; I love to learn and I love to share my expertise. To see others succeed is so rewarding. It takes a village in today's world. Use every resource you need and then give back to other entrepreneurs.

Understanding who people are, where they want to go, and helping them achieve success is lights out!

Authentic entrepreneurs want to give back and bring others along with them. They pay it forward.

10

Entrepre-Mom

If you are a parent, you cannot help but feel a constant tug to be with your children. If you are a professional, you know that you cannot show up for every child activity. You will not make dinner every night at 6 p.m. You may not even be present for each and every holiday event, but you can include your family in the special parts of your life, as my parents did by including me in their work life. As an Olympic coach once told me, you will contribute differently. You will earn enough money to provide your child with an exceptional life with wonderful opportunities, education, and the ability to travel to special places.

I laid a huge guilt trip on my ambitious, hardworking parents. I must have made them miserable on many occasions. In looking back, I realize that as covetous as I was about the way they spent their time, as annoying as I found all the chatter about their business and the attention they lavished on their customers, these were incredible teaching moments for me. By watching my parents at work, I learned the behaviors that helped me find my own place in the professional world. You can provide your kids with a huge gift by pursuing your dreams and showing them how it is done.

My son Brady also experienced what my colleagues called Old Kelly and New Kelly. As you will recall, Brady's father informed me he wanted out of our marriage not long after I awoke from my coma.

I was a single mom for the first time and I needed to learn how to do that. There is no manual on being a good mom; actually there are, tons of them. Each have something to offer but none spoke to me as a multi-tasking mom who happens to be an entrepreneur, CEO of a company and a national speaker; maybe that's my next book, I'll call it Entrepre-Mom.

For me, the best lessons, parenting lessons, came from my family. My grandmother Selma was a rock star as a nurturer and my mother could not be any better. How was I going to do this, and do this well?

My grandmother used to pull me out of high school every week to take me to lunch. She taught me about giving back. My grandmother taught me how to cook. She spent a great deal of time with me. Nothing better than someone who never passed judgment, whether I was in trouble or not (and in my early teenage years, it was more often than not!).

Well, I learned about time management, and I learned about priorities. Brady was three years old when Brian left and he needed a lot of hands-on. I needed a lot of hands-on as well. For the first year and a half when I came home from the hospital, I could not walk up the steps. So Brady slept on the main level on an air mattress. He loved it! It was as if we were having a slumber party every night.

As I was able to get out and about a little bit, but still not back to work full-time, we were able to spend a lot of time together. We took golf lessons, made dinner together, and created snacks and concoctions with smelly stuff from the pantry (which was one of Brady's favorite things to do).

As I got back into the swing of work, Brady often came along. He felt as if he was just another member of the team. Maybe even a supervisor.

One Sunday we ran into Toika, the director of the buyer division, at the Clayton Art Fair. She was there with her family enjoying the day. Brady sauntered up and asked her, "What are you doing here? You need to be at the office." Of course, I was more than a little horrified.

Then there was the time when we went over to Tracy's house to help her and her family decorate their Christmas tree. "Tracy, I love your lights," Brady said.

And Tracy said, "Oh, thank you Brady." Then he went on to say... "My mom doesn't like colored lights. She thinks they're really ugly..." Of course I was horrified once again and said, "Brady, I did not say that."

He corrected me and said, "Yes, you did mom."

Well, maybe. But OUT OF CONTEXT.

Then there was the time that Kim asked Brady to be a ring-bearer in her wedding. He always thought he would be the one marrying Kim, so he was devastated. Brady then wanted to know how much he would get paid for being in her wedding. Horrified again, but have to admire the kid for focusing on profitability.

Brady loves to be the boss. In the beginning when I had my office on the lower level of our home, he considered it his office and would bark orders at Sharon. He did not understand that we were really working down there. We were just his playmates.

At the appropriate times, my staff and their kids enjoyed having Brady and me as their playmates. We called Tracy's husband Joe, super nanny because he had a great way of handling Brady, teasing him just enough to get him back on track when needed. Brady gave the Catchings and Pandolfos an excuse to act like kids themselves when we would all go out together to a playground, a pool or a pumpkin patch.

One thing I learned is that boys are different than girls (it was just my sister Sam and I in our house). If you have a son, I wonder if you've noticed how obsessed they can be with bodily functions. My dad never thought bodily functions were funny. So when Brady was five I told him, "We are not discussing bodily functions while grandpa is in town."

I might as well have handed him a cupcake and told him not to eat it.

On a winter day, my dad gets in the car and the first thing Brady says is "The fart warmers are on grandpa, so your butt won't be cold." We all laughed so hard. Bodily functions. A fascinating and continuing topic of conversation at my house.

It's likely Brady won't remember too much about Old Kelly. That's a good thing. It's not that he was unloved or neglected, but I must confess that I was not always in the moment with my child. I could be with Brady, but thinking too much about work.

New Kelly turned that around. As a working mom, you find the moments and a way to stay in them.

One of my favorite parts of the day is driving Brady to school. School is 45 minutes to an hour away from my house, depending on traffic. It is the only part of the day that we have all of that time together uninterrupted. A lot of mornings we listen to music and dance in the car as only one can when seat-belted in. We are able to talk about life, solve the problems of first grade, and lots of spelling words and math problems. We talk about good behavior and the goals for the day. Be polite, respectful, listen the first time, concentrate and participate.

When Brady was in pre-nursery class there used to be a little girl there that would pick on him and all of the other kids. We called her mean girl Allie. Brady would come home ranting and raving about mean girl Allie, saying that she hit him or another kid in class, or that mean girl Allie had to go to the office again. Can you think of a better way to prepare your kid for a life in the workplace than to talk about people like mean girl Allie and how to handle them?

When it comes to work/life balance, you will find a great deal of literature on how to keep work separate. I suggest it's useful and important to integrate children into your work. That's what my parents did and I am better for it. In doing so, you are setting an example for the next generation in your family line to work hard and smart, to be results driven, to give back to the community, to treat everybody that you work with respectfully and as a member of your family. Participate. Participate. Participate.

Brady participates in a variety of ways, most especially during the holiday season when The Kelly Hager Group adopts dozens of families from Friends of Kids with Cancer. He shops for the kids, he gift wraps, he delivers. It is so terrific for him to be a part of something that is completely for other kids and their families.

Brady isn't the only child involved. All the parents who work for The Kelly Hager Group team bring their children to help at all of our community events. This is what happens when everybody buys in. You just become one big family. We all take care of each other. That is the most rewarding part of being on a team like the one we have built.

The experiences that we have with our kids, whether it's reading bedtime stories, traveling, or helping with Adopt-A-Family, are all great bonding moments. As we got ready for Thanksgiving and were traveling to be with my parents, cousins and uncles, I couldn't wait to spend a great deal of quality time with Brady. Just like when I was a child and would get away from my parents' business life, I know Brady feels the same way.

Top Priority....Build in time away from business life. First annually, then quarterly, then monthly. If you plan for time away, it can be accomplished.

For all you working moms, we might contribute differently, but we contribute a lot. The most impactful memories for both children and parents come from the special events that we share. Thanksgiving week is one of my favorites.

11

The Best Part of What I Get to Do: Giving Back

I have never had a problem asking people for money, especially when it's for someone else.

I also ask people for their time. And, most importantly, their hearts.

I am talking, of course, about community service. I grew up in a middle class home. I have already shared with you how my grandma Selma took me along as she volunteered at Barnes-Jewish Hospital in St. Louis. You should know, too, that my mom, after she retired, got involved in the Make-A-Wish Foundation that provides wonderful experiences to children with life-threatening medical conditions. She also works at a food pantry and teaches art to less-fortunate children in Los Angeles.

So as I watched the people I loved walk in the world, it was natural to want to follow in their footsteps and to make my own mark in a certain way. That commitment grew in high school through my work with the community service club, but grew into an even greater passion when shortly after college I made a trip to Turkey.

I had worked in an English as Second Language program and was fortunate to be invited to Istanbul where I stayed with a family in a beautiful compound in the heart of the city. The family's patriarch was one of the country's leading bankers and his home reflected his success. Just outside his gated entrance, you would find children, many of them apparently orphans, living on the street. These were small children, in need of the most basic items; food, clothing, shoes, a bath, shelter. It was one of those life altering moments for me that I will never forget. I could not blame my host or any particular individual for this dichotomy. I could only look to myself and ask if there was some way that I could repair the world, at least in some small way.

As I flew back to the states, I happened to read an article about how the Xerox Corporation had engaged in an adopt-a-family program. That piqued my interest. One family at a time. That seemed doable.

Over the years, I kept that model in mind as we sponsored a variety of children's sports teams and became active in supporting such causes as The Juvenile Diabetes Foundation and The Leukemia and Lymphoma Society. We also hosted a series of play afternoons for children for Rainbows for Kids, a St. Louis-based non-profit dedicated to helping children with cancer and other serious illnesses.

After a tornado with winds topping 200 miles per hour hit Joplin, Missouri in May 2011, destroying nearly every home, school and business in a path six miles long and nearly a mile wide, our team – then at Keller Williams – jumped in to help. We were in the top 10 market centers out of 700 to raise the most money. Like I said, no problem asking people for money when it's not for me. There are people who donate themselves, and there are people who are a vehicle to help others donate with them. I am that vehicle.

How do you become that vehicle? It's so easy. Choose a cause. Find out the needs. Ensure they match your vision. Go to your top 20 advocates who help you in every avenue of your life. Tell them your plans and ask for their help. Be innovative, take responsibility, and lay out the plan very specifically.

Top Priority......Make a commitment to community. You will learn more in doing this than anything else you do all year. There are challenges, problem solving

opportunities, team building opportunities, opportunities for personal growth, as well as the most important piece which is giving back to the community in which you live. I'm not opposed to just giving dollars, but getting out and being in the community in which you live is really rewarding and is the differentiator.

———

You've heard that rather corny line that when you help someone out, you usually get back more than you give. It wouldn't be said so much if it weren't true. I would like to specify what you get back in a more tangible way. Everyone should give simply because it's the right thing to do. Giving back also creates a culture within your business ecosystem that elevates everyone involved, not just the beneficiaries of your charitable efforts.

A small example. One of my best team members, Sharon, was team manager of a soccer team before she ever came to know me. Sharon wanted the girls on her team to do a community service project as a kind of bonding experience. Sharon went to her friend Tracy, who was then working with me. Tracy had mentioned at one time that our group had gotten involved with Friends of Kids with Cancer. Sharon asked whether the girls could come and help out with that project.

Of course they could, and they did. Sharon got to know me, and it wasn't long before she left a real estate firm where she had been unhappy and joined our group. She liked our spirit and a good measure of that spirit came from our good works. "It's invigorating to be a part of a team that truly gives back to the community. Dollars are one thing, but being able to touch people, face to face, is a cut above," Sharon said.

Sharon, along with every member of our staff, joins in on a whole host of charitable causes supported by The Kelly Hager Group. Most companies do something for the community. I like to think that we are different in that we don't just donate money. We dive in and do things together in a hands-on kind of way as you are now about to see.

Our work with Friends of Kids with Cancer started with one of our team members, Sue. She had a family member who had passed away from cancer, and her family had received help from Friends of Kids with Cancer throughout that period in their lives. Sue introduced us to Judy Ciapciak one day at a frozen yogurt store in 2011.

We had been working with many different organizations, adopting families every year. Judy's organization was helping families one at a time. The organization got started in 1992 when Jill Turec, a developmental specialist at Mercy Clinic Children's Cancer and Hematology Center, Susie Snowden and Molly Henry, parents of children in treatment, came together in the hope of doing what hospitals and doctors could not do – helping with the lives of children and their families beyond the medical treatments.

What Friends of Kids with Cancer does best is listen and then act. When children talked about their rough days in treatment, the Friends created toy closets to cheer them up. When families sighed about how they had to eat the hospital cafeteria food for the umpteenth time, the Friends started Munchie Mondays that provided meals from nearby restaurants like Steak 'n Shake and Subway. As Friends learned that kids in treatment and their siblings were falling behind in their schoolwork, they provided a tutoring program. Friends now provides more than two dozen programs to meet educational, emotional and recreational needs for children in treatment and for their families.

Dr. Bob Bergamini, a pediatric hematologist-oncologist who helped found the organization and serves on the advisory board, said the organization has a unique purpose, "Years ago, curing the sickness used to be the only thing that mattered. Now that so many children are survivors, we have to ensure that the patients and their families are prepared for life after the cancer is gone. Medicine doesn't address these kinds of problems. Friends' programs build self-esteem and improve the quality of life to help kids grow as they should."

Given that mission, who could not fall in love with this organization? They are differentiators for these families. They bring so much value as a support system, and their mission aligns with our mission beautifully. I fell head over heels. To be quite honest, some friends and members of my team thought I had gone around the bend.

We have been doing Adopt-A-Family programs ever since my return from Turkey. Over the last 10 years, we've gotten very serious about helping as many families as we possibly can. I just want to ensure that we can be the vehicle for a successful season in each one of these families' lives.

We used our business acumen and digital prowess to drive the process. We used social media to get the word out and listed each family (without names) and their needs.

High tech and also high touch. Most donors then went out and did the shopping. We then set a drop-off date. Donors would come to our office and deliver their gifts – or even better they would come over to my house where they could pitch in to wrap and sort the tons (I think it was literally tons) of gifts that had come in. We set up folding tables with one table assigned to each family. We cooked up a storm for our generous guests and we dressed up in elf hats and our pink Kelly Hager Group wear.

A few weeks before Christmas, we brought our gifts to the Friends of Kids office and did more sorting and preparation. From there, we would make deliveries to families who could not pick up their gifts. In some cases, we even went to the hospitals with our treasures; nothing more rewarding.

One family that we were able to help last year lived about an hour outside of St. Louis. They had 3 children, both parents worked, and the little boy with cancer was in remission. They were never able to keep their home warm, and their electric bill was more than their mortgage payment in an effort to do so. We reached out to a friend, Adam, who worked at Home Depot (and who now works with us) and they were able to provide that family with insulation for their entire home.

Home Depot is an amazing partner to our organization when we have families in need, and they have gotten even more involved this year. This family was so grateful to have their home warm again, without completely breaking the bank. Making these very small contributions are so beneficial to the families and so rewarding to all of us. It's amazing the help that's out there if you simply ask. Ask, ask, ask.

This year, as one of our team members, Jodi, was leaving our favorite local grocery store, Schnucks, one of the managers was cleaning up from their sidewalk sale, and offered Jodi a sandbox that was left over at no charge. Jodi told her that she personally didn't need it, but that she worked for an organization that supports Adopt-A-Family for Friends of Kids with Cancer, and someone there could use it. She said take it, and we may have some more things for you. The following day, she called and donated 15 jewelry making kits which was awesome. She then offered to donate all proceeds from their Schnucks Fall Festival to Adopt-A-Family as well. That resulted in hundreds of dollars in grocery gift cards that is helping one of our families in need that is literally starving. Another shining example of the community coming together.

In one case our well-meaning efforts seemed ill-timed, at least at first. We were on our way over to a family home with our gifts and called ahead to confirm with the parents that we were coming. As it turned out, their child had died the previous day. We expressed our sorrow and condolences and said that, of course, we would arrange something else.

No way, these parents said. Please come ahead. We brought our gifts, but our gift from this family was to see their grace and presence at a critical time and to understand even better how resilient families of kids with cancer must be in the face of such devastating circumstances.

Each year, we make the effort bigger and better. I can't tell you how much joy this brought to the families. I really can't because I wasn't present for ALL of the gift giving. What I can tell you is how much joy it brought to me and to all our team members. This effort made them feel like they were part of a family, not just a team. It made them feel like their entire lives had meaning and purpose, not just the time spent away from work.

Judy told an interviewer she was "totally blown away" by our efforts. "Not only by Kelly and her passion," she added, "but by her entire team who were doing it from their hearts. Kelly didn't have to make their employees come in. They wanted to do it. They saw the need and wanted to give back. That was what was so moving."

Unfortunately, each year we have had a child that has passed away before we were able to give them Christmas. It's heart-wrenching to understand what these families go through. Seeing the agony, the love, the magic, and the hope that these families endure keeps life in perspective.

So I leave you only with this. What is it that moves you in a compassionate way? Find it. Apply your business skills to the effort. Put your whole heart into it. Enjoy serving. Rewarding beyond your wildest expectations.

12

Connecting the Dots

It's November 5, 2014 and I am engaged in an activity that fills me up. I am at a table in a conference room at Washington University's Olin Business School with five very bright ambitious young women, ranging in age from 22 to 37. A campus organization called Olin Women In Business has asked me to hold forth at a "power lunch" program designed to help students move from academia into fulfilling careers.

I am there for two reasons. I have positions to fill. Looking around the room and listening to their stories, their aspirations and the intelligent questions they ask, I can tell that any one of these women could capably work for The Kelly Hager Group.

The other reason is that I see a little bit of myself in these women and I am here to help them get to where they want to go. Their stories are all different than mine. Though one is close to my age, the others are of another generation. Two are immigrants – one from Asia and the other from the Balkans.

Elaine (I have changed their names here) from China must deal with attitudes that are less flexible and hierarchical than what I grew up with. "I have been told that I am too bossy," she says.

Dora came over from Croatia with her family. Though she was just eight at the time, she was the family translator and had to become assertive in helping her parents navigate in a strange new world. For all of that, she finds as an adult that men expect her to be submissive and they are more challenging when she isn't.

Elizabeth, the eldest in our group, grew up in a typically American home, and sees around her smart women who are married and have careers. Often those careers are subordinated to the men. When they move for a job, the women must pack up too, and find what work that they can. "Can I have a support system, too?" she wonders.

Katharine, who has taken courses in both the School of Architecture and the Business School, finds two different worlds. Architects are used to having women speak their minds. Men in other fields of business aren't. This is disorienting and she has had to adjust.

Here's what I tell them right off the bat. "After all these years and the progress women have made, this is a little surprising to hear. In my business I have surrounded myself with four very powerful women. We all have very strong personalities and we just don't take a lot of that crap."

I encouraged the women at the table to take a step back and look at their lives from 50,000 feet. "The most important teaching that I can give you is to take care of your personal brand. Your personal brand is the team you surround yourself with. It's how you conduct yourself when you are out meeting with people. It's how you communicate with everyone in your office. It is how you conduct yourself in every aspect of your life."

I am imagining that many of you reading this book are a lot like the women who were sitting at that table on a fall day in 2014. If there is anything that I want to leave with you and those women at Olin, it is a sense of possibility. As I said earlier in this book, you can have it all. You just can't do it alone.

Entrepreneurs need the ability to see the big picture, and then connect the dots. First for themselves, then their leadership team, and then the rest of the players on the team. There has to be focus on strategy, but being able to go from strategy to implementation to execution, requires everyone being able to take responsibility and connect the dots.

Let me take you step-by-step through what I have learned as an entrepreneur, as a professional, a woman, and as a mom.

Pressure is a Privilege

It's an honor to be in the position that I'm in today. The last several years I've been so grateful to have the most amazing friends that have turned into family. I will never take that for granted. There is a tremendous amount of pressure from my view, knowing I'm responsible for supporting many families, but I wouldn't change a thing. This is why I get up each and every morning and make sure that we, as a team, excel to the highest level every single day. That's why it's so important that everyone stay in their top 20 percent of critical activities at all times.

Manage your time.

If you have read Steven Covey's *Seven Habits of Highly Effective People*, you may recall that he asks you to sit down every evening to contemplate how you are going to spend the following day. I have gone him one better. I think several days, several weeks out. I am a calendar Nazi.

A nicer phrase is time blocking. The act of time blocking makes me think through what's really important. In my profession, profitability is extremely important. What are the three or four most important activities that I can do in a given day that will enhance profitability?

That's the professional side. If I have learned anything since my illness, it's that you have to invest time in yourself, in your children and family. I schedule time for my son, Brady, with the same foresight and thoughtfulness that I give to my business.

Rest and exercise are critically important to being a high functioning human being. At the same time, great ideas will come to you unbidden as you are closing your eyes or even dreaming. Keep a pad of paper and a pen on your nightstand to write down those thoughts. Otherwise, you may have trouble falling asleep fearing that you will forget your great idea.

One of my best understandings came when I was in the shower, and realized my clients were now my teammates rather than earlier, when my clients were the end consumer. Although that may sound simple, it was very eye opening.

If you're like most entrepreneurs and your passion is strong, "brain dumps" as I like to call them, typically happen between the hours of 1 and 3 a.m., and it's all of the tasks that are going to need to happen in the next 48 to 72 hours. No one likes receiving my emails at 3 a.m. with a subject line of "Brain Dump". Those emails give me so much relief and allow my brain to shut down.

Learn to delegate.

When once I prided myself on being the smartest person in the room, I now realize I don't always need to be the expert on everything. I aim to surround myself with people who know pieces of the pie that I don't understand. Old Kelly had a really hard time letting people do their work the best way they knew how, because she thought she could do it better. In some cases, that's actually true. I might be able to secure a listing or negotiate a contract better than some of our agents. However, all of our agents can do it at least 90 percent as well as I can. That's good enough because it frees me up to do what I really want to do and that which is most important for my role in the company. So you need to land hard on what is the highest and best use of your time and delegate the rest. Easier said than done but the differentiator.

Part of the two way street of loyalty falls to putting in the time up front to really train and develop, so when you do delegate, you're comfortable in doing so. Delegation is definitely one of the most difficult parts of leadership to learn, but it's one of the most important. There's only so many hours in a day, and if you don't delegate your effectiveness goes in the toilet. This can become a huge internal battle, but understanding delegation brings value to yourself as well as your corporation. I have to admit, I do enjoy a good fight with myself from time to time!

On a side note, learning to say "no" can also be challenging if you are the pleaser type of personality, and you do have to do what is best for yourself and your corporation.

Park your mommy guilt at the door.

If you are a parent, you cannot help but feel a constant tug to be with your children. If you are a professional, you cannot make every child activity. You will not make dinner every night at 6 p.m. You may not even be present for each and every holiday event. You can include your family in the special parts of your life, as my parents did by including me in their work life. You will earn enough money to provide your child with exceptional life experiences, unbelievable education and the ability to travel to special places.

I laid a huge guilt trip on my parents. I must have made them miserable. In looking back, I realize that as covetous as I was about the way they spent their time, as annoying as I found all the chatter about their business and as indifferent as I was concerning the attention they lavished on customers, these were incredible teaching moments for me. By watching my parents at work, I learned the behaviors that helped me find my own place in the professional world. You can provide your kids with a huge gift by pursuing your dreams and showing them how it is done.

Most entrepreneurial parents contribute differently. This is not a 9-5 job; it's a way of life.

Find your role models.

Who is it that is leading the kind of life you want for yourself?

For me it was Barbara Corcoran. I want to follow in her footsteps in so many ways. She is financially secure, travels to interesting places, participates in unique activities, and is very busy. That didn't stop me from reaching out to her. You would be amazed at how many people who you perceive to be beyond your reach will respond if you approach them in the right way and ask for their help. People are flattered to be asked. That's human nature.

Once you have made contact, it's important to not waste your role model's time or yours. Bring your brains, come with a methodical approach, ask well thought-out questions, dig deeper and understand why this relationship would be important, and build a great partnership. Being willing to learn and grow is always beneficial. It's the differentiator between a growth mindset and a fixed mindset.

When I am with Barbara I get unbridled candor. I like to think my colleagues are candid with me. I am sure that they are almost all the time, but I am the one who provides them with a paycheck and continued employment, so I have to believe that at one time or another they leave some thoughts unspoken. They are at the very least diplomatic, and when that happens I can fail to pick up on some signals.

There is no problem with Barbara in that regard. She is brutally, breathtakingly frank. It helps that she is a woman, because if a man told me that I needed to airbrush my cover photo, I would probably lose it (actually, I'm still trying to get over that one).

Don't be a five.

A five out of ten is failure; it's less than mediocre. Always strive to be a ten. How are you going to do this? Differentiate yourself. Following up, negotiating fairly, and being committed to your cause, are ways you can either succeed or fail. If you accomplish these tasks with a sense of urgency, in most cases, you will be a ten. If you are slow with these tasks, that spells failure all over it. Consistency and setting the right expectations also leads to ten behavior.

You can always find a way.

We tell our kids almost reflexively that they can be anything they want to be as long as they put their heart and soul into it. This is a lie. I am pretty sure that my son Brady is not going to be the next LeBron, no matter how many jump shots he hoists from our driveway. However, what I want Brady to learn is what my parents, my colleagues, my mentors taught me; there's no problem that you can't solve. Brady is getting it.

Empowergize.

I first heard it from a local marketing company, and I like this word. Empowergize means that you bring drive, direction and passion to your work. You model this behavior for everyone around you. At the same time that you are providing this example, you are depending on your colleagues for their wisdom, their imagination and their direction. You are relying on them to get things done without micromanaging their efforts. You are holding them accountable and at the same time providing them with your time, attention and compassion.

All of this breeds loyalty and trust in your workplace. I work for my team members as much as they work for me. Everyone has to know if we don't work together, we won't be successful. Everyone has to take care of everyone else.

When that happens, you win, and so do we all.

I am really fortunate and slightly lucky. The speed bumps in my life have taught me such valuable lessons. Despite fear and uncertainty, move forward. Your circle of people that surround you mean everything, so get that right. Business life is extremely important and your personal life is equally important. Life is full of choices. Sometimes taking a risk is really important, and sometimes staying the course is really important. Keep the end goal in mind. Life is really short and can pass you by if you aren't careful with your time. Nobody is going to remember you for how many hours you work in a week. Stuff is just that....stuff. Go make a lifestyle full of experiences that mean the world to you and to others. Everything is possible.